Contents

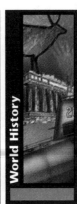

Geography   American History   Government   Economics   World History   Culture

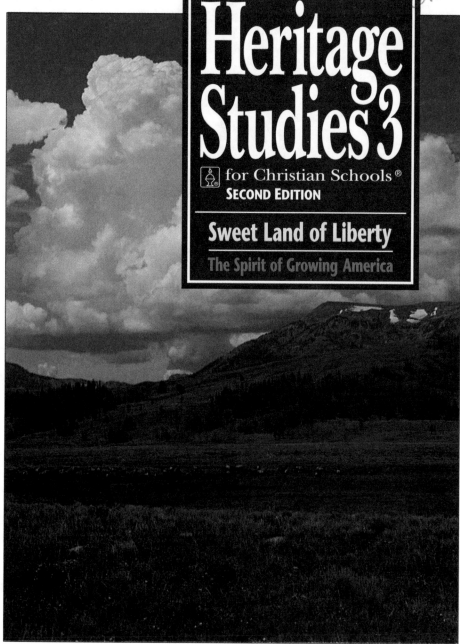

Heritage Studies 3

for Christian Schools®

SECOND EDITION

Sweet Land of Liberty

The Spirit of Growing America

Kimberly H. Pascoe and Dawn L. Watkins

Bob Jones University Press, Greenville, South Carolina 29614

Note:

The fact that materials produced by other publishers may be referred to in this volume does not constitute an endorsement of the content or theological position of materials produced by such publishers. Any references and ancillary materials are listed as an aid to the student or the teacher and in an attempt to maintain the accepted academic standards of the publishing industry.

HERITAGE STUDIES 3 for Christian Schools® Second Edition
Sweet Land of Liberty: The Spirit of Growing America

Kimberly H. Pascoe
Dawn L. Watkins

Produced in cooperation with the Bob Jones University Department of Social Studies Education of the School of Education, the College of Arts and Science, and Bob Jones Elementary School.

© 1997, 1999 Bob Jones University Press
Greenville, South Carolina 29614
First Edition © 1982 Bob Jones University Press

A portion of "I like to see it lap the Miles" (page 166) was reprinted by permission of the publishers and Trustees of Amherst College from THE POEMS OF EMILY DICKINSON, Thomas H. Johnson, ed., Cambridge, Mass.: The Belknap Press of Harvard University Press, © 1951, 1955, 1979, 1983 by the President and Fellows of Harvard College.

Printed in the United States of America
All rights reserved

ISBN 0-89084-931-5

15 14 13 12 11 10 9 8 7 6

1

We the People

New Country, New Problems

The bells of Philadelphia rang as they never had before. The redcoats had given up. America was free of kings forever! People ran into the streets and cheered. They fired their guns. They thanked God for His help.

No one was happier that the war was over than General George Washington. He made sure that all his men were taken care of, and then he went to his home in Virginia.

For a moment it must have seemed as though all the problems were solved. But after the shouts and the gunfire died down, the citizens of the new United States found they did not always get along together.

The leaders in the thirteen states needed to get money. The new country owed money to England and to some American soldiers. The leaders made the people pay taxes. Farmers and shopkeepers and traders had just come home from war. They did not have the money to pay taxes.

The worst sign of trouble was in Massachusetts. The leaders there said that the taxes had to be paid in silver. Some men said, "No! We will not pay in silver! We will fight first!" And they picked up their guns again. But this time they meant to throw their American leaders out.

Shays's Rebellion
Springfield, Massachusetts
January 25, 1787

Daniel Shays got a thousand men to go with him. They all carried muskets, and they all were angry about the taxes.

Daniel Shays said, "You cannot make us pay in silver!"

The governor of the state got a bigger army together. He sent his army to fight Shays's men.

Shays's men lost the fight. They made peace with their neighbors.

The states did not always get along either. Each had its own government. The states were like separate countries, not parts of one country. Something needed to be done. But first, the people wanted to rest from fighting a war.

George Washington wanted to rest too. He said, "I'm going to be a farmer for the rest of my days." But after Shays's Rebellion, his friends came to see him. They said, "You must go help start the new government. If you don't go, the work might not get done. And then all the states will have trouble just as Massachusetts did."

George Washington looked out at his fine fields and his good horses. He wanted to stay home. But if he did, the freedom he had fought for might be lost. The states might get into

fights with each other. Then other countries would try to get American land. He nodded. He had to go.

General and Mrs. Washington in front of Mount Vernon, the home they loved so well

The Constitutional Convention

May 25, 1787

On a cool, rainy Friday morning a group of men took their seats in the State House in Philadelphia. Today we call the building *Independence Hall.* The men's chairs scraped on the wooden floor. Talking and a cough or two echoed in the room. It may not have looked so, but one of the most important meetings in American history was about to begin.

The men had come from twelve states to start a new country—the United States of America. They had come to write laws. They were lawyers and farmers and soldiers and statesmen. Many had been in the War for Independence; many were leaders in their states. They all knew what Americans had given for their freedom. Do you think the men took the meeting seriously?

During the war, the people had lived by laws called the *Articles of Confederation.* That title meant that the rules were to help keep the colonies together. Some of the men thought those laws could be changed a little. Others wanted completely new laws.

Benjamin Franklin was sick that day. But he sent Robert Morris to take his place. Ben Franklin wanted George Washington to be in charge of the meeting. Everyone agreed. Washington was the great hero of the war and a man they all trusted. Washington went and sat in a big chair at the front of the room. The chair had a sun carved on the top of the back.

Then the group chose three men to make a list of rules for holding the meetings. Why do you think they made rules for themselves first? Do you have rules to follow in different places? What happens when you do not follow the rules? What would happen if there were no rules?

This mural painted by Violet Oakley for the Pennsylvania capitol building in Harrisburg shows Washington's chair.

The Mayflower Compact

One hundred sixty-seven years earlier, some other people made rules to live by in a new place. They were the Separatists who came to the New World from England. Do you remember what we call the rules they made for themselves? The rules were the *Mayflower Compact.*

The Separatists brought clothes and food and the Bible. They also brought the idea that they needed the freedom to worship God as they wanted. They also wanted their new settlement to succeed.

The men on the *Mayflower* believed that rules were important. They believed people needed rules to live by. These beliefs "echoed" in the State House of Philadelphia in 1787.

Week after week the men met in the State House. Some days it was hot and big flies buzzed around. The flies bit the men on their legs and necks. Still the men came every day except Sunday to talk about how to run a country. They had many different ideas. If you had been there, what would you have said?

Charles Wilson Peale painted this miniature of James Madison in 1783.

Finally James Madison said, "The Articles will not work any more. We must write a whole new set of laws. We must write a Constitution." The other men sighed. But they knew it was true. They would be away from home many more weeks. They stayed to do the work. They loved their country more than they loved themselves.

June 15

One man said, "I think each state should have one vote in the government." Another man said, "That's not fair! Some states are big. Yours is small. Why should a small state have as much say as a big state?" The first man said, "Why shouldn't it? Shouldn't we all be treated the same?"

Loud voices boomed through Independence Hall. Some men called for a chance to speak. Others argued with those beside them. One man said, "States with more people need more votes. What are you small states afraid of?" Another answered, "Of you greedy big states!" Gunning Bedford of Delaware said, "The big states say they will not hurt the small states. I do not, gentlemen, trust you!"

James Madison listened to the men arguing. He hoped that his ideas for a new government would not be lost. He looked over at George Washington. If you had been in Washington's chair, what would you have done then? Washington frowned a little. The men lowered their voices. But the matter was not settled.

July 2

This day was bright and hot. Some men who came into the hall did not smile. Some of the other men sat in their seats without talking. They had all agreed that the new government should have three *branches,* or parts. One branch would make laws; one branch would see that the laws were followed; one branch would deal with those who did not obey the laws.

The branch that would make the laws had two groups. One was called the *House of Representatives.* The other was called the *Senate.* But the big states and the small states still could not agree about how many votes each state should get in lawmaking. Time seemed to be running out.

President
- Suggests legislation
- Calls special sessions
- Vetoes bills
- Impeaches and removes officials, including the president
- Approves or rejects treaties and presidential appointees
- Overrides vetoes
- Appoints judges
- Grants pardons
- Rules on constitutionality of executive actions
- Interprets treaties

Supreme Court
- Determines constitutionality of laws
- Interprets laws and treaties
- Regulates types of appeals

Congress
- Establishes lower federal courts
- Impeaches judges
- Determines the number of Supreme Court judges

The House of Burgesses

Having two houses in the part of the government that makes laws was not a new idea. In 1619, one year before the Mayflower Compact, Jamestown in the Virginia colony had just such a plan.

The first legislature formed in the New World was in Jamestown.

Jamestown had eleven *boroughs,* or areas. Each borough had two men in the government. The men were called burgesses. The government was called the House of Burgesses. The House of Burgesses had two parts.

Voters elected burgesses to make laws. Who do you think could vote? Only men over sixteen could vote. Can you tell what "echoes" from Jamestown reached Philadelphia in 1787?

July 5

Men from the big states glared at the men from the small states. Then a man got up and offered a *compromise*. A *compromise* is an agreement that is not exactly what either side wants but is good enough for both sides to like. What do you think he suggested?

The man said that in the House of Representatives votes would be given according to how many people lived in each state. Would this idea please the small states or the big states? Then he said that each state should have an equal number of votes in the Senate. Which states would this please?

These girls compromised to make the big sign they will use for their bake sale.

Have you ever had to work out an agreement with a friend? If you have, you probably made a compromise. Compromises are sometimes good. They are bad only if something in the agreement goes against what you know to be right. Would you say the compromise about the votes was good or bad?

July 16

The *Great Compromise* was up for a vote. One man asked how anyone would know how many people lived in a state. Why would that be important? Another said that every ten years the government would count the people, or *take a census*. Has your family ever filled out a census form? It asks how many people live in your house.

Nine states were ready to vote. Five states said yes. Four states said no. The compromise passed by one vote. The men could now write the laws.

The laws are called the *Constitution*. We call the meetings of 1787 the *Constitutional Convention*. What might have happened if the vote had gone the other way?

A copy of the Constitution

Roger Sherman
1721-93

The man who thought up the Great Compromise was Roger Sherman. He was known for being fair and serious. Thomas Jefferson said that Sherman "never said a foolish thing in his life."

Sherman helped write the Declaration of Independence, the Articles of Confederation, and the Constitution. These are three of the most important papers in American history, and he signed them all.

"The words of a wise man's mouth are gracious."
Ecclesiastes 10:12

August 25

The men had worked the whole month of August on the Constitution. They argued over how the president should be elected. They argued over how much members of the House and Senate should be paid. At last they thought the Constitution was ready. Most of the men had been in Philadelphia since May. They wanted to go home.

One man said, "What about the slaves? How can we talk of our freedom and not of theirs?" Another man said, "Slaves are property. They are not important here." The men yelled at each other. Some hated slavery; others did not see anything wrong with it.

George Mason said, "Slavery brings the judgment of heaven on a country." His voice got louder. "God will punish the United States for this sin." Many others agreed with him. But they did not want to talk about it. Why do you think that was? What do you think of Mr. Mason's words?

"For God shall bring every work into judgment."
Ecclesiastes 12:14

The men made another compromise. Slaves could be brought to America for twenty more years. Some men who hated slavery voted for the compromise. Why do you think they did that?

If slavery had been stopped, some states would not have signed the new Constitution. Then the country would have had no government at all. What do you think of this compromise? How is it different from the Great Compromise?

September 17

At last the Constitution was finished. One man read it to the others in Independence Hall. Benjamin Franklin asked all

the men to sign it. Most of the men did. Mr. Mason and two others did not. Ben Franklin looked at the sun on Washington's chair. He said, "That is a rising, and not a setting sun." What did he mean?

The Constitution had a *Preamble* and seven *Articles*. A *preamble* means "words that go before." The Preamble tells why the Constitution was made. The Articles are the main laws that the nation follows.

One law says that the president of the United States must be born in the United States. How old do you think he has to be? He has to be thirty-five. Do you know someone thirty-five? Why do you think the leader is called a president? America is a *republic,* not a country ruled by a king. A *republic* is a government with a constitution.

Another law says that no state may coin money. Why do you think the Constitution says this? What would happen if every state had its own money? It would be confusing.

To Recite the Preamble

1. Take out Notebook page 7.

2. Talk about it as your teacher leads you. Read it with your teacher. Learn the words.

3. Be ready to recite the words for your teacher.

We the People . . .

After the Convention

October 30

Newspapers printed the words of the Constitution. The men who had helped write it made speeches about it. Why do you think they did that? The people of the United States had to know what the Constitution said. They had to decide what they thought of its ideas.

Shopkeepers talked it over with customers. Trappers talked about it to farmers. People talked about it after Sunday church and on busy streets. Soon everyone in the United States had an opinion.

Some people worried. The freedom to have ideas and tell them to others was not mentioned in the Constitution. They thought it should be. James Madison and Alexander Hamilton wrote essays to help people understand that Americans' rights would be safe.

Votes on Ratification of the Constitution

Year	Day	State	Votes For	Votes Against
1787	Dec. 7	Delaware	Unanimous	-
	Dec. 12	Pennsylvania	46	23
	Dec. 18	New Jersey	Unanimous	-
1788	Jan. 2	Georgia	Unanimous	-
	Jan. 9	Connecticut	128	40
	Feb. 6	Massachusetts	187	168
	Apr. 26	Maryland	63	11
	May 23	South Carolina	149	73
	June 21	New Hampshire	57	47
	June 25	Virginia	89	79
	July 26	New York	30	27
1789	Nov. 21	North Carolina	195	77
1790	May 29	Rhode Island	34	32

People said there had to be a *Bill of Rights,* a list of free-doms. They said the list should be added to the Constitution. The leaders said they would add the list after the Constitution was voted on.

Nine states had to *ratify* the Constitution for it to become "the law of the land." What do you think ratify means? It means "to approve of or agree to." What state do you think ratified the Constitution first? It was Delaware.

New Hampshire was the ninth state. What was the second state? What was the last? What day and year did Rhode Island ratify the Constitution?

April 30, 1789

No one doubted who would be the first president. George Washington was the best choice. He was elected and took the oath of office. He repeated the words that the Constitution says each president must say. He said, "I will protect the Constitution."

December 15, 1791

James Madison worked to add a *Bill of Rights* to the Constitution. It says that Americans have rights that cannot be taken away. Do you know what these rights are? Americans are free to worship, speak, gather in groups, and print what they want. They have the right to a fair trial. Nowhere else in the world do people have all the freedoms that Americans have. Why is it good to have these freedoms?

Because he worked on the Constitution and the Bill of Rights more than anyone else, James Madison is called the Father of the Constitution. He helped write the laws Americans live by today. We must be good citizens too. We should learn about our government and help to keep it strong.

2

The Fires
of Freedom

George Washington stood on the balcony of a building in New York City. The people in the streets cheered their new president. He waved back to them. The bells rang out, and guns on ships burst forth with a salute. Americans felt happy. They had a good Constitution. They had a good president. They had a good future.

Across the ocean in France, things were different. It was night in the capital city, Paris. A farmer stumbled through the gates. He was starving and barefoot. "Bread?" he said to a man passing by. "Ha!" said the man. "Where would I get any bread? Only the rich can eat." The farmer dropped to his knees and cried.

A shopkeeper sat up late in his house. "You can't get married," he said to his daughter. "I have no money to pay the marriage tax. I can't even pay the tax on this salt." He shoved a small dish away. Suddenly he stood up and his stool fell back on the floor. His face got red. "The king has taxed away all the money I ever had!"

The king was Louis XVI. His grandfather, Louis XV, had been the last king. Louis XV spent more money than he had. How do you think he got more money? He made new taxes for the working people to pay. What do you think he did with the money? He bought things for himself and sent soldiers to fight for land in the New World. How do you think the French people felt?

Louis XVI

Louis XVI knew the people had not liked his grandfather. Do you think he tried to be a better king? Someone told him, "The people are unhappy." Louis XVI said, "I'm sorry. Really. Bring me my horse in the morning. I want to go hunting."

Queen Marie Antoinette looked at herself in a long mirror. Her dress had gold threads in it. It shimmered in the light. She wanted always to live in the beautiful palace and wear pretty clothes. "You are still beautiful," her maid told her. Marie Antoinette smiled.

Marie Antoinette

In the streets of Paris a baby cried. The mother had no food and no money to buy any. Nearby a group of men talked about the Americans. "They have their own government. They do not pay taxes to a king! We should do as they did." "Shush!" said another. "We'll be thrown in jail!"

The men glanced toward the jail. It was called the *Bastille*. Everyone had heard of the terrible things that happened to people in there. Anyone who spoke against the king might be put in a dungeon with rats and spiders—or worse.

In another town, workers stormed into a factory. They were angry that they did not make enough money. They broke down the doors and tore down walls. Then they burned the factory. Do you think that any of these actions helped them?

The king's soldiers rushed to the town. The people ran into the houses. They threw stones and flowerpots at the soldiers. They tore tiles off roofs and threw those. The soldiers fired their guns. Many people died. At last the fighting stopped.

A week after George Washington had become president of the United States, the French king made a decision. Louis XVI said, "I will meet with the leaders of the French government." What do you think he wanted to talk about?

There were three parts to the French government. There were the church leaders, the rich people, and the people who had to work, like shopkeepers, farmers, and servants. Which group do you think wanted the taxes to be lower? Which group do you think wanted bread to be cheaper?

The leaders of the three parts of the government went to see the king. The king came out of the palace to talk. The churchmen wanted the taxes to stay high. Why do you think that was? Churchmen did not pay taxes. Some of the money from taxes went to the Roman Catholic Church.

The rich people wanted the taxes to stay high. The rich people also got some of the tax money paid by the townspeople. The rich used the money to buy more things for themselves.

What do you think the common people wanted to do about taxes? What do you think King Louis wanted to do? The meeting went on for weeks. Why do you think it took so long? The shopkeepers and the cloth makers and others said, "We speak for more people than the other two groups. We should have more votes in the government. And the king should not have so much power."

Then the king said, "I will not change things the way the workers want. I am the king. Go away and come back tomorrow." The rich people left. The churchmen left. The townspeople did not move. The soldiers in the back held up guns with bayonets on them. But the shopkeepers and farmers and others did not leave.

The leader of the townspeople said, "We take no orders." Someone told the king, "The poor people are not leaving as you told them to." "Well," said Louis, "then they can stay." What do you think of the king's answer? What do you think the people thought of it? They thought that now they were more powerful than the king.

Marquis de Lafayette
1757-1834

Not all the rich people tried to keep the common people from having more votes in the French government. One of the most important nobles who liked the common people was the Marquis de Lafayette.

Lafayette had fought with General Washington in the War for Independence. He was a general. He commanded American soldiers. General Washington thought of Lafayette as his son. Lafayette brought many French soldiers and much French money to America. He helped the Americans win the war.

Lafayette told King Louis XVI that the common people should have a part in the government. He said, "The government used to listen to the people." Later Lafayette changed his mind about what the common people were doing.

In some towns, poor people were hungry. Sometimes they robbed the bakers and the millers. If the people thought some-one was storing food or grain in his house, they would break in to get it. What do you think of these actions? It is wrong to steal, no matter how good the reasons may seem.

The streets of Paris were always full of people. If a cart turned over, hungry people rushed to grab up any food that fell out. Men whispered together in shops. "The Americans do not live like this. I fought in their war. Now they are free." Another man said, "Be careful. Do you want to live in the Bastille?"

The people of Paris did not like the Bastille. It stood for the power that the king had over them. Big cannons loomed out from it. Soldiers guarded it. The people thought that anybody who could not pay taxes was held there.

A man got up on some steps. He said, "Why should we fear the Bastille? Let's go there and make the governor take the cannons down!" The crowd cheered. "Let's go!" they said. And they went, hundreds and hundreds of people.

"Take down the cannons!" they said. "Give us guns!" The governor peeked out at the mob. He ordered his men to take down the cannons and to board up the openings. Still the people were not happy. "Let us in!" they said. "Give us guns!" "No," said the governor.

What do you think the people did then? Do you think they went home? They smashed their way into the Bastille. They wanted to free all the prisoners. How many prisoners do you think there were? There were only seven. Then the mob killed the governor.

Unknown 18th-century French artist, Taking of the Bastille, July 14, 1789, Arrest of the Governor, Monsieur de Launay, *©PHOTO Réunion des Musées Nationaux*

King Louis XVI came in from hunting. He had not gotten any deer. He went to bed. He did not know what had happened at the Bastille that day. What do you think happened when he found out?

The king ordered his soldiers to march to Paris. The soldiers went. But a surprising thing happened. The soldiers did not fire their guns at the people. The soldiers joined the people. Now the king did not have soldiers he could trust. If you had been King Louis, what would you have done?

Declarations of Independence

The French common people put themselves in charge of the government. They called their government the *National Assembly.* "Now," they said, "*we* will make the rules for France."

The National Assembly wrote a paper to tell the people what the new government believed. The paper was called the *Declaration of the Rights of Man and of the Citizen.* It said that everyone should have the same rights. It said that the king should not have all the power.

Do you remember an American paper that said such things? The Declaration of Independence did. The United States Constitution also did. Ben Franklin had the Constitution written out in French. The French people read the Constitution. Some ideas from the American war "echoed" in the French Revolution.

The National Assembly offered to let King Louis stay as king. "You will have to give up some power," the leaders told him, "but you can live in your palace and be called the king." Do you think Louis should have taken the offer?

The royal palace of Versailles

Queen Marie Antoinette said, "Don't listen to the people. I don't want to give up power. Tell them you are still the king." Louis told the people what the queen wanted him to.

The people were angry. "Things will not go back to the way they were. We want change! If the king won't hear us, we'll throw him out."

"Better is a poor and a wise child than an old and foolish king."

Ecclesiastes 4:13

Paris, France
January 21, 1793

King Louis XVI was put on trial. He was found guilty of being against the revolution.

"Off with his head!" the people cried.

He was taken to the *guillotine*, a machine that lets a heavy blade drop from high up.

A few months later, Marie Antoinette was also taken there.

Kings and queens in other countries were shocked at what had happened to Louis XVI and Marie Antoinette. They said, "That might happen to us. Our people might get bad ideas from the French." Some kings and queens sent armies to France. Some wanted to stop the French Revolution. Others wanted to take over France.

The French people began to fight among themselves. Some thought that the king should not have been killed. Leaders of the revolution arrested people who were not on their side. Many of those people went to the guillotine.

"No one is safe," said a baker. "Keep your voice down," said his wife. "Tell me," said the baker, "haven't we only traded one terror for another?" The whole next year was called *the Terror.* How was the revolution in France different from the American War for Independence?

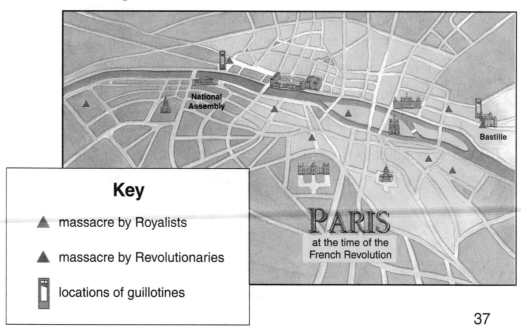

Key

▲ massacre by Royalists

▲ massacre by Revolutionaries

▯ locations of guillotines

National Assembly

Bastille

PARIS
at the time of the French Revolution

People wore red caps and scarves to show they were *revolutionists*. Why do you think they did that? They wanted the leaders to see they were on the right side. Some people who were not revolutionists wore red ribbons around their necks. What do you think the ribbons showed? They showed that the person knew someone who had died on the guillotine.

The leaders of the revolution got an army together. This army fought the armies of the other countries that came against France. The army also fought the French people who did not like the revolution.

The soldiers in the new army did not have much training. But they wanted to fight. That made them able to win many battles, even when the enemy had soldiers who had been in many wars.

Making Up National Songs

A man in the new French army liked to write songs. He wrote a song for the soldiers. He thought it would cheer them up and help them march better.

The mayor of a small town sang the song first. The soldiers and the people liked it. Soon everyone was singing it. It was called "The War Song of the Army." It said, "The day of glory now is here. Let us march! Let us march!"

Later the song was named for a town the soldiers marched from and became the *national anthem.* What is a national anthem?

To Find and Chart Facts

1. Get a pencil and Notebook page 12. You will also need a set of encyclopedias.

2. Find the names of the national anthems of the countries listed. Find the date that the French national anthem was adopted.

3. Write the names of the anthems in the blanks.

Some Americans wanted to help the French people fight their enemies. They said, "The French helped us. We should help them." But others said, "We have just started our country. We should make America strong before we fight for France."

If you had been George Washington, what would you have said? Washington thought of Lafayette. Then he thought about the new United States of America. America had just come out of a war. He said, "I think we should not get into another war."

"You're wrong," said Thomas Jefferson. Washington said, "It is wrong to risk our new freedom. France was a strong, old country during our war. And the French were enemies of the English. We are just beginning a nation. And France's enemies are not our enemies." America stayed out of the French Revolution.

Napoleon, *painted by Jacques-Louis David*

The French soldiers won many battles. The generals became famous and important. One general won a big battle against the English. He became a French hero. His name was Napoleon Bonaparte.

Napoleon won more battles. The revolution ended in 1795. A group of leaders tried to run the French government together. Then in 1804, Napoleon took his soldiers to Paris. "Make me head of the government," he said. "Or I will have the soldiers fire on the city." The people made Napoleon the head of the government.

Napoleon said, "You people do not know how to run a country. I will put things right for you." And he did make many good changes. But Napoleon made hard rules for the people. Some people began to wish France still had a king.

Jacques-Louis David, The Emperor Napoleon in His Study at the Tuileries, *Samuel H. Kress Collection, Image © 2004 Board of Trustees, National Gallery of Art, Washington*

3

From Sea to Shining Sea

What if you could travel anywhere that you wanted? Where would you choose to go? What things might you see there? Of course, we cannot all go anywhere in the world. But we can learn about the places we would like to see. Maps can tell us some things about those places.

What kinds of things do maps show? Some maps show streets and buildings. Some maps show towns. Others show where one country ends and another country begins. Are these the only things maps show us?

Maps show us man-made things like roads and cities. And maps show us things man did not make. The things man did not make are called *physical features*. Who made these physical features?

"*The sea is his, and he made it: and his hands formed the dry land.*"
Psalm 95:5

Here is a map of the world. What things does this map show? It shows water. Water is blue on a map. The earth has four large bodies of water. What are these bodies of water called? They are *oceans*. Can you find all four oceans?

Most maps show land too. Big areas of land are called *continents*. How many continents do you see? There are seven. Each one has high land and low land. But all the continents are different too. Can you think of some ways in which they are different?

This map of the world also shows how the continents are divided. It does not emphasize land features such as rivers, lakes, and mountains.

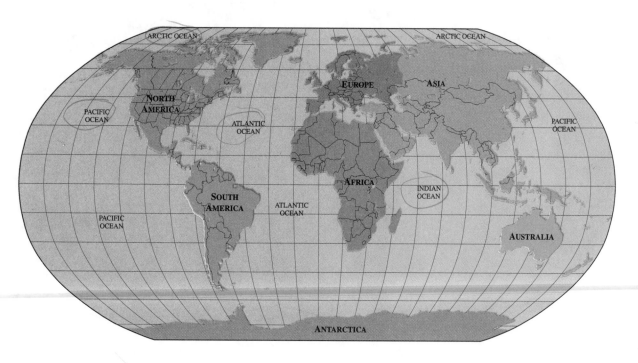

This map is a special kind of map. How is it different from the map you just looked at? It shows some of the physical features of our world. Maps like this one are called *physical* maps.

This physical map shows some of the rivers and lakes on six continents. Which continent does not have rivers and lakes? Other physical maps show different physical features. What other features might a map show?

Can you find the continent called North America on this map? America is part of this continent. How many rivers and lakes do you see? Do you think this map shows all the rivers and lakes?

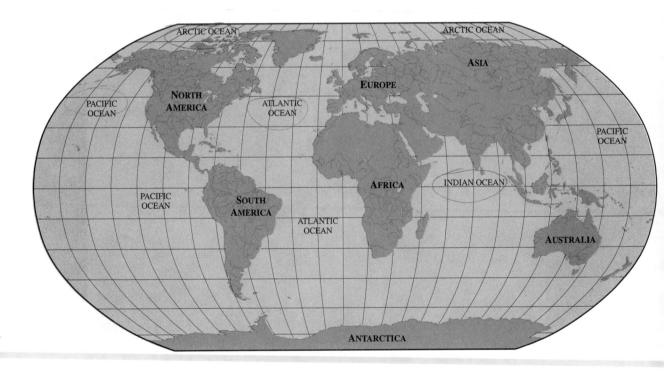

To Read a Physical Map

1. Get a large physical map of North America.

2. Turn to the physical map on pages 284-85. Look at the map key. A map uses different colors to stand for different things. What do the colors on this map stand for?

3. Now look at the map. Find the state you live in. What color is it on the map? Is the land in your state high or low? What other physical features does your state have? Compare the map in the book to the large map. How is it the same? How is it different?

The United States is a big country. If you traveled across the country, what things would you see? Would the land look the same in each place you went?

The Big Forest

Long ago, the land between the Atlantic Ocean and the Mississippi River was a huge *forest*. A forest is a place where many trees grow. Can you find the land that the forest covered on the map on page 49?

Not many people lived in the forest. But it was full of many kinds of animals. Look at the pictures of animals from the forest. Can you name them? What other animals might have lived in the big forest long ago?

How did the people who first came to America travel from place to place? Some people said that the forest was so thick that a squirrel could go from the Atlantic Ocean to the Mississippi River without ever touching the ground. It was hard to travel through such a thick forest.

Most of the time, the people traveled on *rivers*. A river is a large stream of water that flows across the land. Can you find any rivers on the map? Rivers are shown as thin blue lines.

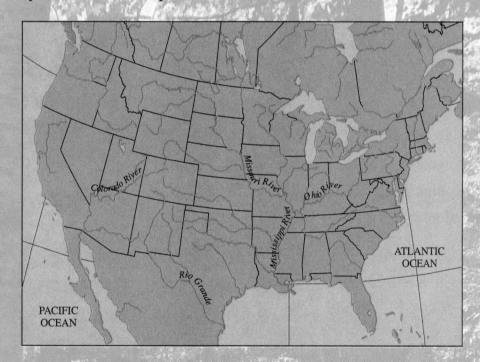

Today some of this same land is still covered with forests. But most of the land is not. What other things would you see instead? Farms, small towns, and even big cities cover the land. Which of these places would you like to visit?

The Wide Open Prairie

Beyond the wide and muddy Mississippi River, the land is different. It is flatter. Few trees grow there. Some people liked this flatter land, or *prairie,* better than they liked the forest land. Once they passed the trees along the riverbank, they could see for miles.

What things do you think the people saw on the prairie? First they saw grass. Some of the grass was as tall as a person. When they looked closer, the people saw other things too. They saw little animals, like prairie dogs and badgers, that lived on the prairie. Do you think these small animals saw the people? They did. And they ran to their underground homes to hide.

The people saw another kind of animal on the prairie. It was not like any animal they had seen before. The *bison* was the biggest animal on the prairie. One person told about a very big *herd,* or group, of bison. It took three days for that herd to pass. What kind of noise do you think such a big herd of bison made?

At one time, people thought that nothing but grass would grow on the prairie. They called the prairie the *Great American Desert.* Were these people right? Later they found out that the prairie soil was very rich. Farm crops grew well there.

This picture shows part of the same land today. How has the land changed? What do you think caused the change? More and more people came to live on the prairie land. They planted crops and trees. Today it is hard to believe that people once called this land a desert.

Snowcapped Mountains

Those people who crossed the wide prairie saw hills steeper and taller than any they had ever seen. Land that is much taller than the land around it is called a *mountain*. The Indians called these the "Shining Mountains." Why do you think they gave them that name?

Today we call these mountains the *Rocky Mountains*. Settlers had crossed much lower mountains in the East. Can you find these mountains on a map? The eastern mountains were not so steep and rocky. They were not covered with snow all year round either.

High in the mountains, the air is colder than it is on the prairie. It is too cold for most plants to grow. Do you think any animals can live there? A few can. Look at this animal. What would you call it? It is a bighorn sheep. Bighorn sheep live high in the Rocky Mountains.

Desert

Hot, dry, dusty, and brown. These words make many people think of just one thing—a *desert*. A desert is a place that gets only a little bit of rain each year—less than ten inches. Some deserts are scorching hot too. But other deserts are cold. Antarctica could be called a desert. Lack of water makes living in the desert hard.

Even though deserts are very dry, the land is not bare. What kinds of plants can you see in a desert? Do you think any animals can live there? God gave the plants and animals that live in the desert special ways of staying alive. Plants like the cactus have long roots that draw water into special storage places in the plant. Some cactuses can hold more than one hundred gallons of water. Animals get water when they eat these water-holding plants.

By the Beautiful Sea

The mountains and the deserts stopped some people from moving farther west. Do you think that it was impossible to cross the deserts and mountains? It was not easy, but many people found a way.

Look at the map. Can you tell what these settlers found to the west of the mountains and deserts? They reached a thin strip of forest land. And beyond the forests, they found the *coast*.

The coast is the land at the edge of an ocean. We also call this land the *shore*. There are many different kinds of coasts. Some coasts are wide, sandy beaches. The ocean water rolls gently over these beaches. Other beaches are not so wide. Those beaches are filled with pebbles and shells. A third kind of coast is very steep and rocky. There the ocean water roars and crashes against the steep shore. Have you ever seen one of these kinds of coasts?

Traveling Across a Continent

North America is 2,807 miles wide from ocean to ocean. Have you ever traveled that many miles? Why did you make the trip? Some people travel that many miles every week. They make trips across the continent for different reasons.

Sometimes people want to see all the special places in their country. They might take weeks or even months to travel. People on a business trip zip across the continent in just a few hours. And some people even walk or ride a bike across their continent. Would you like to do that? How long would it take to ride a bike two thousand miles?

Today we have many ways to travel across a continent. But that was not true many years ago. In those days, a person could travel by boat on rivers. He could ride on a horse or in a wagon pulled by horses or oxen. Or he could walk. Which way would you have chosen to travel?

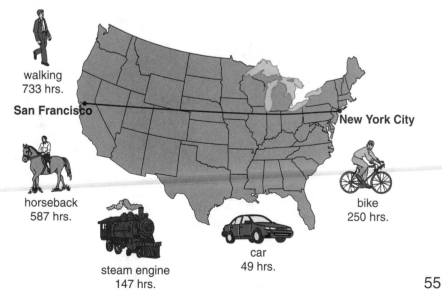

walking
733 hrs.

San Francisco

New York City

horseback
587 hrs.

bike
250 hrs.

steam engine
147 hrs.

car
49 hrs.

Exploring America

Thomas Jefferson held the letter in his hand. It was from his messenger to France, James Monroe. What would the letter say? Did Napoleon, the ruler of France, want to sell the city on the Mississippi River?

President Jefferson could not believe what the letter said! Napoleon had agreed to sell New Orleans. But that was not all. He wanted to sell all of Louisiana. James Monroe bought all the land for the United States. Now his little country was twice as big as it had been.

What was the Louisiana *Territory,* or area of land, like? No one really knew. But the president wanted to find out. He wanted, too, to make friends with the Indians in the territory. President Jefferson had already picked someone to lead a group of explorers. He asked his good friend Meriwether Lewis.

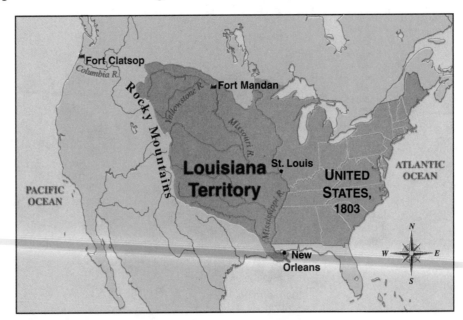

Meriwether Lewis planned carefully for the trip. His friend and assistant, William Clark, helped him. Together the men bought food and boats for the trip. They bought goods to give to the Indians as gifts of peace. And they chose thirty-one men to go with them.

The men left St. Louis on May 14, 1804. That summer they pushed and pulled their loaded flatboats and canoes up the Missouri River. It was hard work. Along the way they met many different groups of Indians. The men gave each chief a silver medal with President Jefferson's picture on it. They gave the other Indian people bracelets, cloth, and tools. The Indians promised to be the white men's friends.

Some of the Indians that they met had never seen white men before. They had only heard of them. But none had seen or heard of anyone like York, Clark's strong black servant. York would just laugh when the people tried to rub the "black paint" off his arms.

Lewis, Clark, and the men spent the winter near the Mandan Indian village. They built a fort and named it for the Mandans. "My wife and I can help you find your way," a man who came to visit Fort Mandan told Lewis and Clark. "I have traveled farther on this river than any other white man. And my wife is an Indian. Her people live in the Shining Mountains."

Lewis and Clark were not sure that they wanted to take a woman with them. She might make them travel more slowly. But they needed someone with them who could speak the language of the Indians in the Shining Mountains. The two men agreed to let the little family come along.

Soon the ice in the river began to melt. The group left Fort Mandan in canoes carved from trees. The Missouri River was not very wide, and the water flowed swiftly. They left behind the big flatboat and some of their supplies.

Sacajawea

A baby girl was born into the family of Eagle Chief. The chief named her *Sacajawea,* "Bird Girl" in the Shoshone language.

Each fall Sacajawea's people left their mountain home. They traveled many miles to the edge of the prairie to hunt bison, or buffalo. Why do you think they hunted this animal? One year the herds of buffalo were small and hard to find. The Shoshone went far onto the prairie to hunt.

Then the Shoshone's enemies attacked! The enemy braves captured Sacajawea and made her a slave. She worked hard for her new master. But she missed her people in the mountains. She hoped that someday she would go home.

Years later Sacajawea, her husband, and her baby son joined Lewis and Clark at Fort Mandan. Sacajawea was a great help to the white men. She knew which herbs to use for medicine. She knew which plants and animals were good to eat. And she helped Lewis and Clark buy horses from her people, the Shoshone.

As the men came closer to the Shining Mountains, traveling was harder. The river got smaller and faster. Sometimes it was so fast that they could not float on it. Then they carried the boats and supplies.

Soon the group needed horses. They could not cross the mountains in a canoe. And if they tried to walk across the mountains, they would get caught in the winter snowstorms. Lewis set out to find Sacajawea's people.

Lewis left gifts for the Shoshone to find. When he met the Shoshone, he used the signs and Indian words Sacajawea had taught him. The Shoshone chief sold horses to Lewis and let an old Indian go with him to lead the men across the mountains.

Beyond the mountains, the traveling was easier. They built new canoes and floated quickly down another river. Then one foggy day they heard a steady crashing sound. As the fog cleared, the men knew they had reached their goal. They had reached the Pacific Ocean!

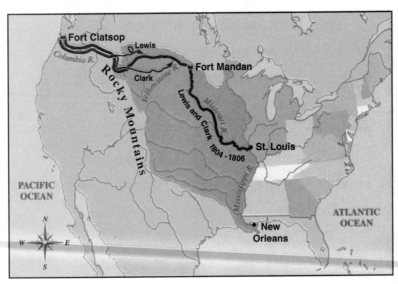

St. Louis
September 23, 1806

This day was a day for celebrating. Meriwether Lewis, William Clark, and their men had come back to St. Louis.

The men had been gone two years, four months, and twelve days. Most people thought that they all had died in the wilderness.

But Lewis and Clark had had good guides. They traveled all the way to the Pacific Ocean and back. Their journey took them more than eight thousand miles.

Imagine the things these men had seen! They would have many exciting stories to tell for years to come.

Today North America stretches from ocean to ocean. It covers all of the land that Lewis and Clark saw on their adventure and much more. It is a beautiful land of snow-covered mountains and grassy hills, deep, dark forests and sandy coasts. What parts of America do you like best?

"Thou art worthy, O Lord, to receive glory and honour and power: for thou hast created all things, and for thy pleasure they are and were created."

Revelation 4:11

4

The American Frontier

Starting to Go West

Daniel Boone had tramped through deep woods and crossed many streams in his day. He had seen flocks of pigeons so thick that they blocked out the sun. He had heard the screams of bobcats; he had listened to the strange animal noises coming from the swamps. But not even Boone dreamed what was beyond the Appalachian Mountains.

Few settlers believed the tales the Indians told of huge trees and giant bears in the West. Few people believed Lewis and Clark, who reported millions of bison on the plains. They did not believe John Colter, who said there were great spouts of water in the Rockies and a lake so deep that it seemed bottomless. Today we know all about grizzly bears and redwoods and geysers. But try to imagine how wild all the stories must have sounded to someone in Franklin's Philadelphia.

Philadelphia had wide streets paved with stones. It had shops and brick houses. It had street lamps and a fire company. Sometimes pigs and cows wandered down the sidewalks. And now and then someone threw garbage out his front door. But most people thought Philadelphia was the best city in the world. What do you think the other big cities were like?

Giant redwoods

Castle Geyser,
Yellowstone National
Park, Wyoming

City life was not for everyone. Many people wanted to get to the open space of the West. At first, only the brave and strong went. They lived on what food they could find along the way, slept on the ground, and made clothes from the skins of animals.

Sometimes a man went out on a trip and did not come back for years. Such men were called *long hunters*. Why do you think they were called that? What do you think they were hunting for? Some were looking for land to farm. Some were looking for furs to sell. Some were just looking to see what was out there.

fur cap: the result of his marksmanship

homespun shirt: big square pockets to hold dried meat

handmade buckskin jacket: coat for protection against rain, cold, snow, and thorns

shot pouch: holds ammunition and occasionally other items such as new laces for boots

leather pouch: holds a compass, a tool made of bone, and perhaps a needle for repairing clothes

rifle: weapon for protecting himself and getting food

homemade boots or moccasins: sturdy protection for the journey of hundreds of miles

James Beckwourth
1798-1866

The young man wiped the sweat from his face and then pumped the blacksmith's bellows again. But all the while he thought of the wide prairies and the Indians that the traders had told about. A few months later he set off with some traders into the wilderness.

James Beckwourth soon became a good shot with a rifle and a friend of many Indians he met. He learned to track animals and to find food anywhere. Still he nearly starved to death one winter in the mountains. Just in time, a band of Kansas Indians found him and took him in. He was chased by bears; he was shot once; he nearly drowned in a flooded river.

Beckwourth made many trips west. He became a scout for the army. Then he built a trading post near the gold mines in California. He went out looking for gold himself—and found something more important. He found a *pass,* an easier way over the Rocky Mountains. Why was the pass a good find? It saved many from starving in the mountains. Today that pass, a mountain, a valley, and a town in Nevada are all named for the black pioneer Beckwourth.

After the long hunters came back with stories and advice, other people started moving west. They followed the trails the long hunters had followed. How do you think the stories of the long hunters helped them? The long hunters told where to find water, where Indians lived, where the trails were dangerous.

Still the going was not easy. Some Indian tribes did not want the white man to cross their land. Some shot arrows at settlers and burned the wagons. The travelers fought back. They thought the land did not belong to anyone. Why do you think they thought that?

Most Indians did not build permanent cities. They moved from place to place during different times of the year. They took only what they needed from a place. They did not "wear out" the land by staying too long. Settlers did not think about that. They said, "There are no houses here. No barns. This land is free for the taking." What do you think of that idea?

Daniel Drake was just a little boy when his father and mother went west to Kentucky. Do you think they had a place to live when they got there? They lived in a sheep pen until Mr. Drake could build a cabin of logs. Have you ever seen a log cabin?

Daniel's father laid the logs together as tightly as he could. He cut a notch in the ends of the logs so that the logs would fit snugly. Daniel could still see light between the logs. What do you think Daniel's father did about the cracks? He may have filled them with mud or clay or moss or all three.

The roof was made of boards and wooden slabs called *shakes*. Inside the cabin, the floor was dirt packed down hard. There was only one door with a heavy bar across it. The Drakes kept a rifle on the wall and an axe under the bed. They wanted to be ready for anything.

To Build a Model Log Cabin

1. Get some toy building logs or some craft sticks. If you are using sticks, you will also need a felt-tip pen, scissors, an empty milk carton, construction paper, and some glue.

2. If you are using the logs, build a small cabin. Make sure the notches fit together. If you are using the sticks, use the pen to mark notches at the ends. Glue construction paper onto the sides of the carton first. Then build your cabin.

3. Make a roof with the pieces from the log set or in the way your teacher shows you. Do you think log cabins were comfortable to live in?

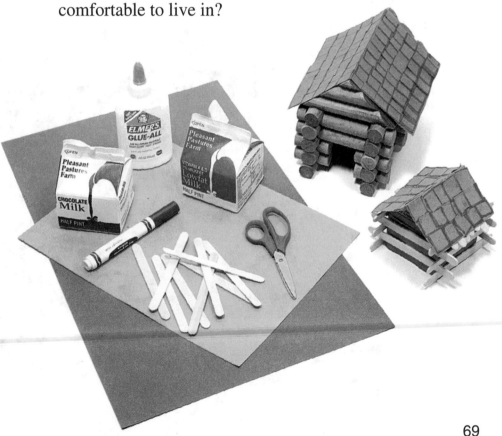

Food around the Drakes' cabin was easy to find in summer. Turkeys perched in trees and deer filled the woods. Daniel's mother picked berries and wild plums. The first winter the Drakes ate mostly meat, so much meat that Daniel cried for some bread.

The next summer Daniel's mother planted pumpkins, turnips, beans, and—most important—Indian corn. She made a sweet syrup from some of the pumpkins and dried the rest. The turnips and beans went into the cellar. Putting up the corn for the winter was more fun.

In places where neighbors lived fairly near, harvesting the corn became a *frolic*. Everyone came to help husk the corn. After all the work was done, they sat down to a dinner and joked and told stories until late at night.

What kind of people do you think settlers were? Do you think they were scared and weak? Do you think they did whatever anyone said to do? Pioneers worked hard. They made rules to live by. They knew how to do things for themselves. Do you think Americans are still like the pioneers in any way?

Another War

England and France were fighting a war. England wanted to take Napoleon out of power. English sailors who did not want to fight the French sneaked onto American ships. They hid on the ships. England found out what the sailors were doing. What do you think the English did then?

English captains stopped American ships and searched them. English sailors on American ships had to go back to their own ships. How do you think Americans felt about having their ships stopped and searched? They were angry!

President Thomas Jefferson made all American ships stay home for a year. Many Americans thought that rule would solve the problem. If no ships were sailing, no ships would get stopped. Others thought that President Jefferson was afraid of fighting.

Henry Clay did not like the plan. He said, "We should tell the English to stay off our ships!" He told the other members of the government what he thought. "We should fight England!"

James Madison became president after Jefferson. What do you remember about Madison? He agreed with Henry Clay. About twenty years after the War for Independence, the United States went to war again. English ships sailed up the Potomac River to Washington, D.C. The English soldiers set fire to the president's house and the new Capitol.

Washington, D.C.
August 24, 1814

President Madison sent word to his wife. "Leave the Capitol! The British are coming!"

Dolley Madison looked around. "Well, they won't get my china! Nor these papers and books!"

She packed up trunks with important letters, silver, and other things. Then she hurried out. She passed by a picture of George Washington. In a flash, she cut the picture out of the frame and took it with her.

Today we have many treasures from the early days because Mrs. Madison thought fast and acted quickly.

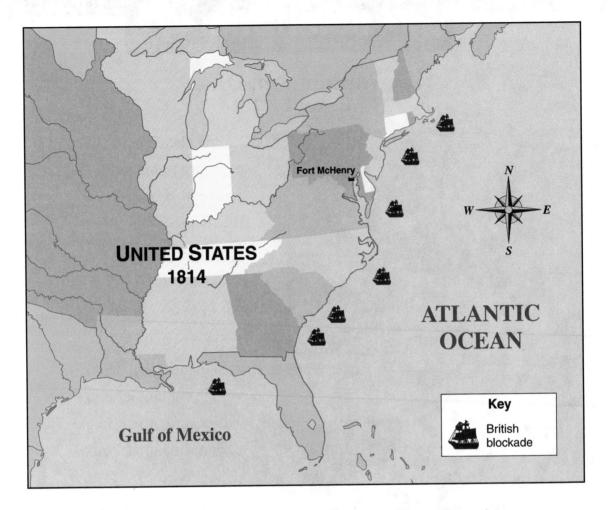

English ships kept American ships from sailing. Sometimes the English ships fired cannons at towns and forts on the coast. They fired on Fort McHenry. The cannons of the fort fired back. All night the guns roared. The blasts lit up the sky like lightning. People in the fort did not know what would happen.

If the English won, they would take down the United States flag and put up their own. Every time a cannon blast lit up the night, Americans tried to see which flag was flying over the fort. What do you think they saw?

Writing an Anthem

One man near Fort McHenry watched the United States flag at every bomb blast. When the sun started to come up, he strained to make out the stars and stripes on the fluttering cloth. "Please," he thought, "let it still be the American flag."

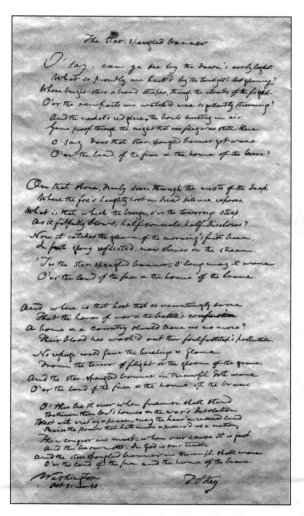

He took out a pencil and began to write a poem. It was a poem that asked the important question, *O, say, does that star-spangled banner yet wave?* When the sun was up, he had his answer. The United States flag was still there.

Francis Scott Key finished his poem the next day and put it in his pocket. Do you think it stayed there? No, it later became the words of our national anthem. We call it "The Star-Spangled Banner." What other national anthem do you know about?

To Sing "The Star-Spangled Banner"

1. Listen as your teacher reads the words of "The Star-Spangled Banner." In your own words, tell what these lines mean.

2. Sing the anthem along with the recording. Try to imagine that you are watching for the American flag at Fort McHenry with Francis Scott Key as you sing.

3. Learn the words to the first verse of the anthem as your teacher helps you.

The war was called the *War of 1812*. But the war lasted more than one year. At first England won most of the battles. Then America began to win. America hoped to take Canada from the English. Why do you think America wanted Canada?

For one thing, Canada had lots of beavers and foxes and otters. Hunting was good there. Americans also wanted to get the English off their borders. Americans still remembered the War for Independence. And they did not want the English to rule them again.

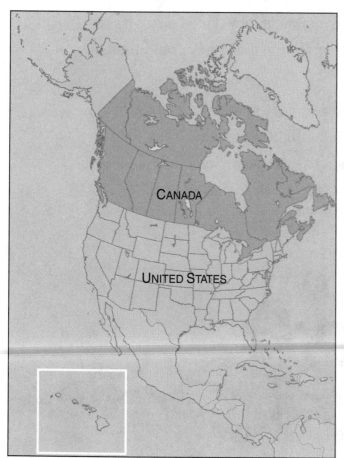

The War of 1812 ended with a treaty. The people of the United States were proud. They had proved that their country would defend its rights. Did the United States take Canada? No, Canada still belonged to England.

Modern political boundaries of the United States and Canada

More People Go West

The first people to cross the Appalachian Mountains got a big surprise. They were used to deep woods and hills and rough roads. Suddenly the land flattened out in every direction. It looked like an ocean of short bluegrass. The prairie seemed like a whole new country. In the beginning the travelers thought, "This will be much better for travel."

The land was flat, but water was not always easy to find. And there were no *landmarks*—easily seen objects like mountains and trees—to go by. How do you think the people kept going in the right direction? Every night they turned their wagons toward the North Star. In the morning, then, they could figure out which way west was.

Sometimes the oxen or horses got too weak to pull the heavy wagons. Then the settlers had to lighten the load. They left behind organs, trunks, cupboards, and beds. Sometimes children had to leave their toys. How would you feel about that?

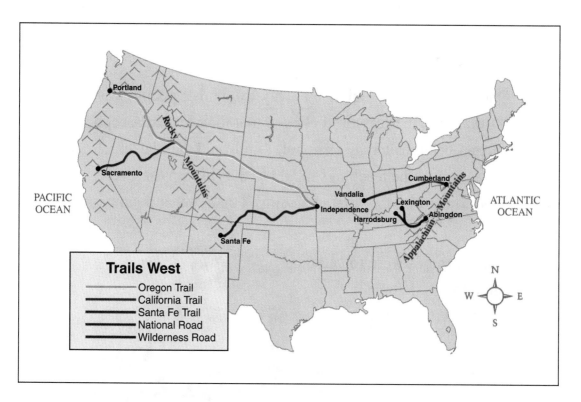

Trails West

- Oregon Trail
- California Trail
- Santa Fe Trail
- National Road
- Wilderness Road

Most settlers followed the same trails. The trails had names like the *Oregon Trail,* the *National Road,* and the *Wilderness Road.* Can you find these trails on the map? What do the names tell you about the trails?

For a few years the people going west were like a small stream. Then the people and wagons became like a river. Why do you think people went west? Some wanted more land. Some wanted to get away from problems where they were. Some wanted to be left alone to live as they pleased.

The Mormons

One group that wanted to get away from other people was the *Mormons.* The Mormons believed that their leader, Joseph Smith, had been visited by an angel. Smith said that the angel had given him some teachings to add to the Bible. Wherever the Mormons went, the "extra teachings" made other people angry.

The Mormons were forced out of all the towns. People in one town burned the Mormon houses and killed Joseph Smith. Another man took over. He said, "We'll go west. We'll stay on land no one else will want."

Joseph Smith, the first Mormon leader

Modern Salt Lake City, Utah

The Mormons crossed the prairies. They came to a dry, ugly place. The lake was salty. "This," said the new leader, "is the place." He told the settlers to dig ditches to bring water from the mountains to the flat land. He told them to build houses and plant trees. In a few years the Mormons made a green farmland out of a desert.

The place they settled in is now Utah. For a long time, Utah could not become a state. The Mormons had to agree to give up some of their ideas. They still believe that they can get to heaven by belonging to their church and doing good works. They believe that everyone is good. What do you think about these ideas?

The Trail of Tears

One group of people was forced to go west. They were the Cherokee and other Native Americans from the South. White settlers wanted the Cherokee land for big farms called plantations. Also, someone had found gold on the land. The government told the Cherokee that they could have land in the Oklahoma Territory. The Cherokee had to go.

Thousands of people packed up all their goods. They left their homes and land. The United States government told them not to worry. "We will give you food. We will help you." But the government did not do what it had promised.

The Cherokee walked for months, in the winter, over rough land, without enough food or blankets. Children got sick. Old people died. Soon many of the strong began to starve. They got smallpox. The people called their trail the *Trail of Tears.* Those that lived set up villages on a *reservation,* a place set aside for Native Americans.

Robert Lindneux, The Trail of Tears, *Woolaroc Museum, Bartlesville, Oklahoma*

Mountain Men

Some people traveled by themselves. Fur trappers and hunters lived alone in the Rocky Mountains. Sometimes they would not see another person for months or years. They were a tough breed. One man, Peg Leg Smith, once hurt his leg badly. To keep from dying, he cut off his own leg. He was famous ever after.

When the mountain men wanted to trade their furs, they met at a *rendezvous*. At the planned time, dozens of them came out of the mountains to the Great Salt Lake. Indians came. Owners of fur companies came. The trading went on for weeks. The fur companies gave guns, gunpowder, food, and traps for the furs.

Missionaries and Preachers

Missionaries often were the first white people in a new place. The Whitmans and the Spaldings traveled across the prairies alone. They climbed the Rockies. Fur trappers helped them find their way to Oregon. Narcissa Whitman and Eliza Spalding were the first white women to see the Pacific Ocean.

The missionaries went west to tell Indians about the love of Christ. When more settlers came, the missionaries sometimes became leaders of churches too. Why do you think most people wanted to travel in groups? Why do you think missionaries did not always wait for wagon trains?

A circuit-riding preacher as shown in the film Sheffey *(Unusual Films)*

Most new towns did not have a preacher. So one man would be the preacher for several towns. He would ride from one town to the next on a planned route called a *circuit*. Have you heard of circuit-riding preachers? In summer several preachers held *camp meetings* together. Lots of people came to hear preaching, to sing, and to visit with neighbors.

"How then shall they call on him in whom they have not believed? and how shall they believe in him of whom they have not heard? and how shall they hear without a preacher?"

Romans 10:14

A camp meeting scene from the film Sheffey *(Unusual Films)*

Camp meetings of long ago were a little like evangelistic services of today—and quite a lot different. As in today's services, the goal was to get people to turn from sin to the Lord. And many of the songs we sing in evangelistic meetings now were sung then. Perhaps you know "On Jordan's Stormy Banks" or "Brethren, We Have Met to Worship."

But the camp meetings were not just in the evenings. They began with prayers at five o'clock in the morning. After breakfast there was singing and preaching until noon. After lunch there was more singing and preaching. At night the services were mainly singing and a different kind of preaching called *exhorting. Exhorters* talked to the people. They begged them to come forward and be saved.

The camp meetings went on for several days. Many families lived in tents or wagons for the week. Often at the end, people cried when they had to leave. They were fond of the place where they had been saved. And they had become good friends with each other.

California Bound

In 1846 America fought another war. This time it was with Mexico, the country to the south. America won the war. Can you find on the map the land America got from Mexico after the war?

John Sutter built a fort in the newly won land. He gave food and shelter to weary travelers coming west. He built his own mill and shops and put up houses for all the people who worked in the fort. In 1848 something happened that made Sutter's Fort famous around the world. What do you think that was?

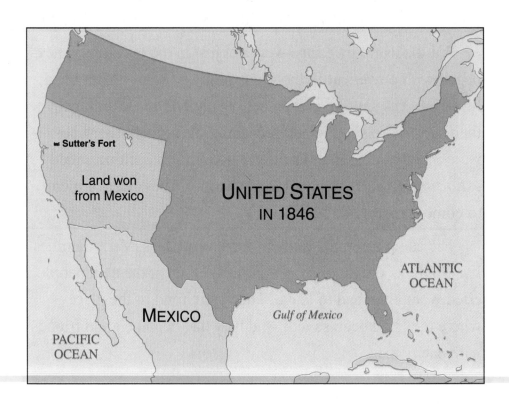

A Mill at Coloma, California
Spring, 1848

John Marshall was hired to build a mill for John Sutter. Marshall began his work on the American River. One morning he went walking along the river.

He said later, "My eye was caught by a glimpse of something shining in the bottom of the ditch." That "something" turned out to be gold! Sutter's Fort would never be the same. What do you think happened next?

Sutter wanted to keep the gold a secret. But word got out. In a year, thousands of men came to find gold in California.

Sutter's Mill

Advice to Gold Seekers

"Never Travel on the Sabbath; we will guarantee that if you lay by on the Sabbath, and rest your teams, that you will get to California 20 days sooner than those who travel seven days a week."

—from *The Emigrants' Guide to California,* a pamphlet for gold seekers traveling to California in 1849

The *gold rush* of 1849 brought gold miners from back east. It also brought them from England, France, Germany, and Ireland. They came by the pioneer trails. They came by ship. They called themselves *forty-niners*. They came and came and came. San Francisco went from two thousand people to twenty thousand people in one year.

Men set up tents and shacks and went right to the river to pan gold. They worked all day, day after day. Many who came were thieves; many were wicked men who would kill for money. Even among good men, fights started over gold dust. A few men got very rich. Many made some money. A lot more went home with nothing or died crossing the desert on the way.

Lots of people stayed in the West. They built farms and started families. California became more famous for vegetable farms and fruit orchards than it had been for gold.

5

Stories from Long Ago

Once upon a time, people liked to tell stories around camp-fires or at tables after dinner was over and after the chores were done. Of course, people still like to tell stories today, and many stories they tell are the same stories people told long ago. Do you have a favorite story that you like to tell or hear? Maybe it was loved by people hundreds of years ago too.

We can learn about the people who lived long ago by listening to the stories they told. Some stories tell us what the people believed about the world around them. Other stories show us things that the people were afraid of or things that they wished for. Still others teach us about the ways people got along together.

Parables

Sometimes a story taught a lesson. We can read in the Bible some of these kinds of stories. Do you know what they are called? They are *parables.* Parables are usually about people.

Parable of the Lost Coin

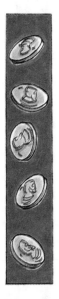

Either what woman having ten pieces of silver, if she lose one piece, doth not light a candle, and sweep the house, and seek diligently till she find it? And when she hath found it, she calleth her friends and her neighbours together, saying, Rejoice with me; for I have found the piece which I had lost. Likewise, I say unto you, there is joy in the presence of the angels of God over one sinner that repenteth. (Luke 15:8-10)

Fables

Often storytellers would tell a lesson-story about animals instead. The animals in these stories acted like people, and each animal always acted a certain way. For instance, Fox was always tricky and Owl was always wise. How do you think a bear would act? Stories that teach a lesson through the things animals do are called *fables.* The Cherokee told this fable. Do you think the lesson it teaches is important today?

The Game

The Animals wanted to challenge their friends the Birds to a contest. But what kind of contest could they have? All the Animals thought and thought. "We can have a ball game," said Deer, who could run faster than any other Animal.

The Birds accepted the challenge, and when the chosen day came, they met on a grassy meadow near the river. The Animals chose Bear to be their chief because he was the biggest and strongest. The Birds chose Eagle as their chief, for he was the bravest.

The goal poles were in place and a good ball was ready. But before the game began, the players practiced together. Turtle beat the drum, and all the Animals practiced in the meadow. They bragged, too, about how they would surely win the ball game. Each reminded the others that they were faster and stronger than the Birds.

The Birds, practicing in the treetops, did not brag like the Animals. Eagle Chief told the other Birds, "We may not be as big and strong as the Animals, but we will play hard. We must do our best."

Just as the practice time was over, a tiny creature came to Bear Chief. "I am an Animal," he said. "I have four legs like all the other Animals. And I would like to play ball on the Animals' team."

Bear Chief laughed and laughed. "You are too little to play on our team. We are big and strong, and we do not need help from creatures like you."

The creature was very sad, but he did not give up. He went to Eagle Chief. "I want to play ball. Will you let me play on your team?"

When Eagle Chief heard this story, he felt sorry for the tiny animal. He called all the Birds together. "This creature would like to play ball on our team, but he cannot fly. What can we do?"

Now the small creature was very, very sad. "Don't be sad, for we can help you," said Hawk and Falcon. "Look here what you have on your sides." And they took hold of the skin on his sides and pulled. They said, "You have wings of a sort!" He said, "I am Flying Squirrel!"

It was time for the game to begin. The ball flew high in the air, and Hawk caught it. He passed it to Falcon. Falcon flew toward the poles. But then he dropped the ball!

Just as Bear Chief was about to grab the ball and run with it, Flying Squirrel swooped down and snatched the ball away. He glided between the poles. The Birds had won the game, and the Animals had never even touched the ball.

Never be sure that you will win, just because you are bigger or stronger than those you play against.

Legends

Sometimes a favorite story might be about things that happened to a real person. But each time the teller told the story again, he told it a little differently. After many years, no one could be sure how much of the story was true. Stories like these are called *legends*. Read this legend of John Chapman. Do you know of other real people whose life stories became legends?

Johnny Appleseed

John Chapman was born on a farm in Massachusetts about the year 1775. Johnny was a good boy who loved his parents and the rest of his family. He always thought he'd stay right where he was, helping his father on the farm. He would have too if he hadn't seen all those people headed west.

Hundreds and hundreds of people, in wagons and on horseback, passed by his father's little farm. Why were they going west? One day Johnny decided it was time for him to find out for himself what was so great about the West. So he packed his belongings, said good-bye to his mother and father, and headed for Pittsburgh, which was about as far west as most people went back then.

Johnny didn't have much trouble deciding what to do when he got to Pittsburgh. He bought himself a piece of land, and he planted the thing he loved to tend to best: apple trees. His trees were strong and sturdy, and his apples made the best-tasting apple cider, apple pies, and apple dumplings around.

Soon Johnny saw that not every wagon stopped in Pittsburgh. Some people traveled even farther west. When he thought of all those people, living in the wilderness with no apples to be found anywhere, he felt he would cry. How could a person live without apples?

Johnny knew what he should do. He carefully saved and dried each seed from the apples he grew. He made little bags from deerskin and filled each bag with apple seeds, and he gave a bag to every wagon that passed his farm. Soon everyone was talking about that kind man, "Johnny Appleseed," who gave apple seeds away.

Still Johnny worried. Not everyone knew how to care for apple trees like he did. They might plant the seeds and never bother to care for the little trees, or worse yet, they might not ever plant the seeds at all. He hated to think that his good apple seeds were wasted that way. So he thought of a new plan.

Johnny sold his farm. He sold almost everything he owned. Then he loaded his apple seeds into a canoe and paddled down the Ohio River and into the wilderness. He would plant apple trees for the settlers in the West, and he would tend to them too.

People thought Johnny Appleseed was crazy, and you might have thought so too if you had seen him. The longer he stayed in the wilderness, the funnier Johnny looked. When his shirt wore out, he cut holes in a potato sack for his arms and his head and wore it instead. He lost his hat to a bear one night, and after that he took to wearing his cooking pot on his head.

Although the people laughed at Johnny at first, the laughing didn't last long. Soon Johnny was the favorite visitor in every camp and settlement in the West. He knew more about living in the wilderness, curing sicknesses, and, of course, raising and eating apples than anyone else. And he always had a good story to tell. The best stories of all were the ones he called "the good news from heaven," which he read from the big black Bible he carried everywhere.

Johnny spent the rest of his days in the wilderness planting apple trees. Forty years after he left Pittsburgh, he died in a little apple orchard in Indiana, his Bible lying open by his side.

Writing Stories Down

For many hundreds of years, parents and grandparents remembered and told stories like "The Game." Few people could read or write, so the stories did not need to be written down. As more and more people learned to read, they realized that it would be good to have a written copy of some of these old stories.

Two of the first people to think of collecting stories in books were brothers named Jakob and Wilhelm Grimm. They listened to stories told by the people near their home in Germany. Then they wrote 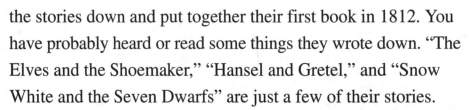 the stories down and put together their first book in 1812. You have probably heard or read some things they wrote down. "The Elves and the Shoemaker," "Hansel and Gretel," and "Snow White and the Seven Dwarfs" are just a few of their stories.

Later, people in other countries began to write down their old stories. Missionaries in the West helped the Indians write their fables and myths. People still write down many different kinds of stories. Some of them are stories they have heard from other people, and some are stories they made up by themselves. We call people who write stories *authors*. Do you know any authors?

Folktales

Folktales are another kind of story told long ago. Many different kinds of stories can be called folktales. A folktale might tell about a lovely princess or a kind prince. It might tell about a brave hero who slays giants and monsters. Most people wished that they could be a princess or a hero like their favorite story character. Some folktales told funny stories about everyday happenings or about animals. Funny stories like these helped the people to forget the hard things in their lives. "The Gingerbread Man," "Sleeping Beauty," and "Little Red Riding Hood" are folktales. Can you think of any others?

The Alligator and the Deer

Long, long ago, tweren't nothin' around here but birds and animals and Indian men. Some animals, they get along. Some animals don't. Deer and Alligator not be getting along. Alligator want to kill Deer first chance him gets.

'Fore long, the new man comes to live here. He the white owner. He bring along he hounds to hunt Deer. Those hounds so fast when they chase Deer. He just as 'fraid of them hounds as he is of Alligator.

White owner's hounds are onto Deer. Him only chance to get away is to run in that water. But he know who in the water waiting for him. He sees Alligator's eyes. Deer is stuck. Those hounds is hungry. Alligator is very hungry. What Deer to do?

Just in time, Deer turn to the side. He run down the riverbank away from them hounds and Alligator. But the hounds don't know what he did. They don't see Alligator, either. Three of them run right into the water, and they land smack in front of Alligator.

"What this?" Alligator think to himself. "I not seen these things before, but they look good to eat." And he had heself two of them hounds for dinner. Then he takes a little rest.

Soon Deer comes to the water. He needs a drink after he hard run. "Hey, Deer," Alligator calls. "Them things they call hounds is very good to eat. They easy to catch and they got no horn to scratch my throat when I swallow. I want to eat them all times. Let's us make a 'greement."

"What kind of 'greement you thinkin' of?"

"Just this," answered Alligator, "When them hounds be chasin' you, just run for the water. Then I'll eat the hounds which's after you."

So Deer 'greed. And when hounds take to chasin' Deer, he heads for the water. Alligator leave he alone and gets them hounds. But when Deer come to the water without the hounds be chasin' him, he have to take he chances.

Tall Tales

People told fables, legends, and folktales in many countries all over the world. But one kind of story was heard only in America. People who told *tall tales* stretched the truth. In fact, tall tales are full of outright lies. The bigger and more impossible the lies, the better the story is.

Almost every worker in America knew about a tall-tale character who did the same kind of work as he did. Cowboys, lumberjacks, sailors, and riverboat men all had their favorite tall-tale hero. This tall tale is about an unusual steel worker.

The Best Steel Man

Steve Mestrovich's daughter was the prettiest girl in all the world, and even in all the Monongahela Valley. So of course, Steve knew that she must have the best husband around. To Steve, who was a hard working steel man, the best man meant the strongest man.

"I will hold a contest," Steve told Mary. "The strongest man will be your husband."

The day of the contest arrived. The young men came from town and all over the Monongahela Valley. One by one they tried to lift the heavy steel bars as Steve and Mary watched. "I hope that Pete Pussick wins," thought Mary. "He is the one I want to marry." It looked like Pete would win too. But that changed when Joe Magarac showed up.

Never before had anyone in all the Monongahela Valley seen Joe Magarac. He was something to see. He stood taller than the trees in Steve Mestrovich's yard. His legs and arms were as big around as oak trees. His

hands were big as shovels. And he was so strong that he picked up all the steel bars and Pete too!

"You are the strongest man in the world, and even in all the Monongahela Valley," declared Steve. "You will make the best husband for my Mary. Who are you?"

"I am Joe Magarac. Ho, ho, ho! Mary, you are the prettiest girl I ever seen. But I don't need a wife. What I need is a job. I'm the only real steel man in the world, or the Monongahela Valley even. See!" And with that he rolled up his shirt sleeve a bit, and everyone saw that his arms were made of shiny steel.

Steve Mestrovich gave Joe a job right there, and the next day he started work at the steel mill. It usually took eight men to run one of the huge furnaces, but Joe Magarac could do all the work by himself. When the steel was ready to be made into rails, he picked it up in his hands and squeezed it out between his fingers, eight rails at a time. He was the best steel man in the whole world, . . . but Mary married Pete anyway.

The stories that people told long ago in America came from many countries. They tell us about many different kinds of people. The stories tell us about the hopes and dreams, fears and humor of the "normal" people. They remind us that even though not everyone was a hero, everyone wanted to be.

To Write a Tall Tale

1. Get your notebook paper and a pencil. Prepare the paper as your teacher tells you how to form a long, narrow writing sheet.

2. Read and select a story starter that your teacher suggests or think about something you would like to do. It might be a job or a sport you like to play. What would help you do that thing better? What if you were taller or shorter? What if you were made of iron, seashells, or rubber? Remember, the more impossible a tall tale is, the better the story.

3. Write a tall tale using one of the story starters or telling about a person who can do the job or play the sport you chose. Tell about the funny and impossible things that happen to this person. Share your tall tale with your friends. Why do you think people like tall tales so much?

6
The
United States

Regions of the United States

Choose a state and look at the map. Which section of the country is the state in? Why do you think it is in that group? What is one way that states are put into groups?

The United States can be divided into six groups of states. Find the Northeast, Southeast, Middle West, Southwest, Rocky Mountain, and Pacific regions on the map. Do the names of the groups give you a clue about how the groups are divided?

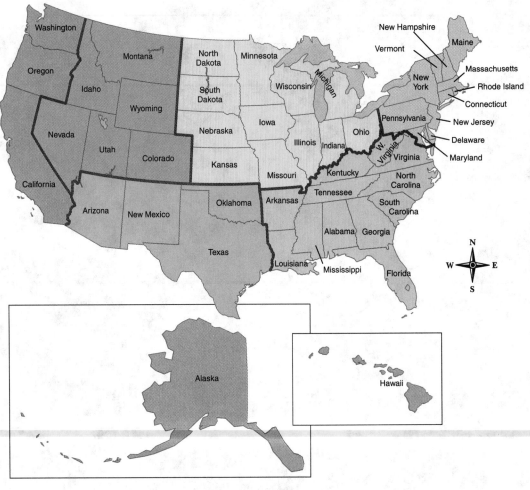

The Northeast

Reconstructed Separatist settlement

What do you remember about how this area was settled? Who were the first comers? They were the Separatists from England. Where did they settle? What groups settled Pennsylvania? German farmers and people called Quakers were some of the first settlers. Can you name some important events that happened in this region in America's early history?

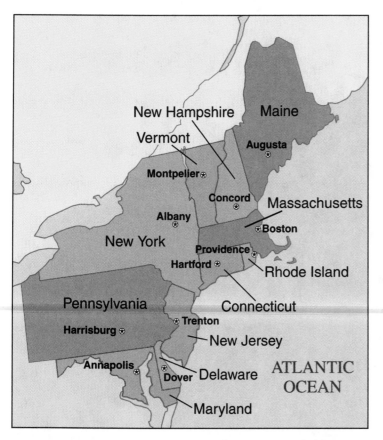

What states are in this region now? Can you find the capital cities of the states? How are they shown on the map? Look at the map of the Indian nations on the next page. Before the white man came, who had lived in the northeastern section of this land?

111

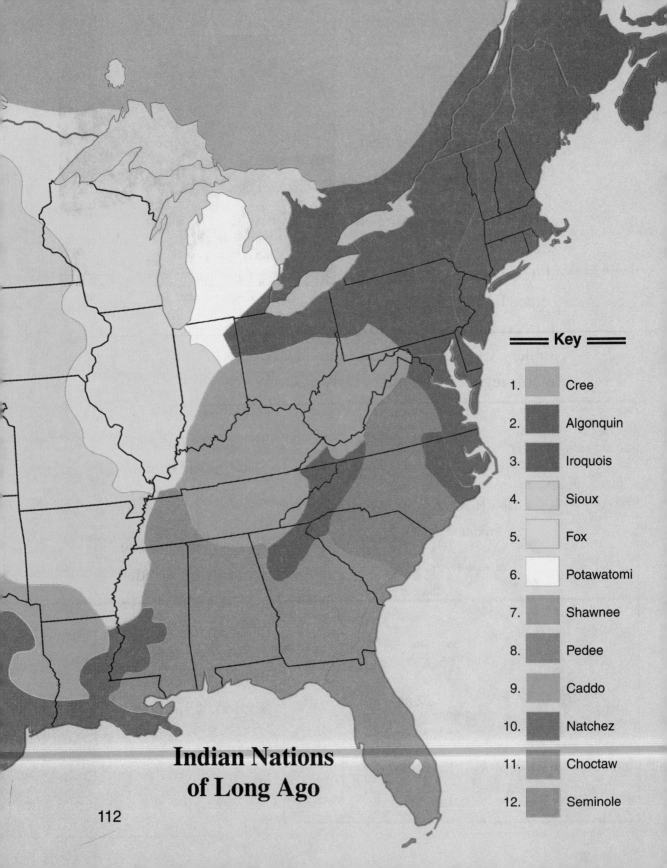

Key

1. Cree
2. Algonquin
3. Iroquois
4. Sioux
5. Fox
6. Potawatomi
7. Shawnee
8. Pedee
9. Caddo
10. Natchez
11. Choctaw
12. Seminole

Indian Nations of Long Ago

Vermont gets its name from the two French words *vert* and *mont.* The words mean "green mountain." What does the name tell you about the state? Can you guess Vermont's nickname? It is "the Green Mountain State."

One nickname for Massachusetts is "the Bay State." A *bay* is a body of water that is nearly circled by land but has a wide opening to the sea. Look at the map on page 111. Can you tell why Massachusetts has the nickname it does?

The Northeast has many good *harbors,* safe places for ships to dock. The better the harbor, the bigger the town grows beside it. Which cities seem to be on the best harbors? The Northeast settlers built fine ships. Today many of the harbors are still busy.

New York Harbor

The Southeast

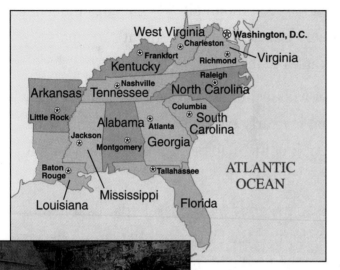

Look at the map on this page. How many states are in the Southeast? What are their capital cities? Does the Southeast have good harbors? Charleston, South Carolina was an important harbor. Can you find it on a map?

Reconstruction of a home in early Charleston

Do you remember which state had the first English settlement that lasted? It was Virginia. What was the name of the town? It was called Jamestown, after the English king James I. The people who came to Jamestown were hoping to find gold. What they found instead was a place to grow tobacco. Soon they began to grow tobacco to send to England.

Now look at the map on page 112 to find the names of the people who lived in the Southeast before the Jamestown settlers arrived. Which group also lived in the Northeast?

Many places in the Southeast grew cotton. Growing cotton was hard work. Workers had to hoe the ground between the cotton plants. Hoeing kept the weeds down. Then the cotton had to be picked. Some landowners made *slaves* work in the cotton fields and in their big houses. A slave is a person who must work for someone without getting paid.

Can you remember the problem that came up in the Constitutional Convention about slaves? Some members of the convention wanted to let slavery go on. Some wanted to stop it. Do you remember what happened? People were allowed to bring slaves to the United States until 1807. Do you think slavery stopped after that? No, it did not.

A slave family on a plantation in the South

The Middle West

Some people from the East felt crowded in their cities. They wanted to move west. Soon after the American War for Independence, settlers swarmed into what is now Ohio. At that time it was part of the Northwest Territory.

The explorers Lewis and Clark went to look over the Louisiana Territory. Who asked them to go? They were among the first white men to see much of the land we now call the Middle West, or Midwest. How can you find out what people lived in the region when Lewis and Clark passed through?

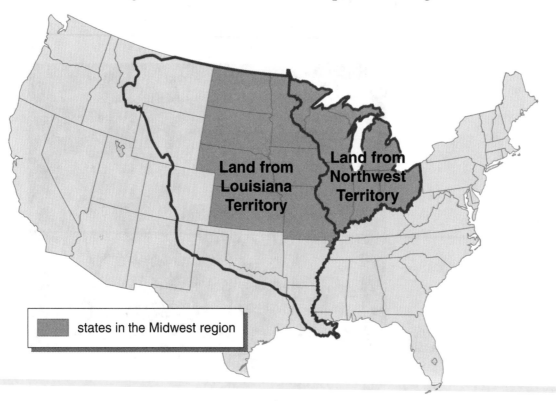

Land from Louisiana Territory

Land from Northwest Territory

states in the Midwest region

Which Midwest state borders the most other Midwest states? How many others does it share a border with? By looking at the map on this page, can you tell how some state borders are decided? What rivers make borders?

Other state borders are decided differently. Do you notice how many of the midwestern states have straight borders? Could these borders have been made along rivers? How do you think they were made?

Sometimes people agree that a line should divide land into states or counties or farms. Since the line is not actually drawn on the ground, the people hire a *surveyor* to decide where the border is.

> *"Thou hast set all the borders of the earth."*
> Psalm 74:17

Surveying

A *surveyor* is someone who measures land and helps decide where borders are. He uses special tools to make the measurements.

The most important tool is called a *transit.* It is a small telescope. It sits on a three-legged stand. A line with a weight hangs down from the transit. It marks the very middle of where the transit sits.

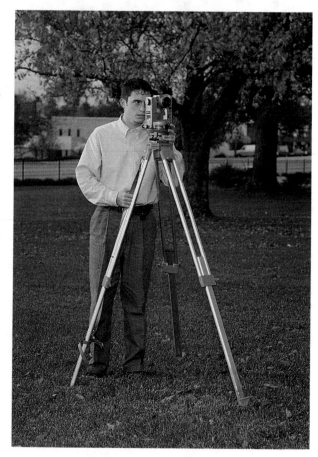

If the surveyor knows that the border needs to go north, he aims his transit north. Then a helper can measure from the weight on the line to the point that the surveyor tells him.

George Washington was a surveyor in Virginia. He used a special chain to measure with. Today surveyors use calculators, computers, and photographs taken from airplanes in their work.

The Southwest

Almost at the same time that Columbus was landing in San Salvador, other explorers were marching into the Southwest. These explorers wore iron helmets and rode horses.

Coronado was a Spanish explorer who was looking for the Seven Cities of Gold. He had heard stories about rich lands to the north of Mexico. He searched and searched. When he did

not find gold, he punished the Pueblo people he did find. What do you think of his actions? Look at the map on pages 286-87 to find where the Pueblo people lived for hundreds of years before the men with the iron helmets came.

A reenactment of the Coronado expedition

What four states make up the Southwest? What are their capitals? Santa Fe is the oldest capital city in the nation. It was founded in 1610. Had the Pilgrims arrived in the Northeast yet? No, they would not come for another ten years.

Irrigation is bringing water from a river or lake to the fields. Since much of the Southwest gets little rain, farming depends on irrigation. The Hohokam people had used irrigation hundreds of years before the white man came. In the 1860s a white settler studied the old Indian town and built ditches like those he saw there. Soon many farmers nearby used the irrigation plan.

A town called Phoenix grew where these well-watered farms prospered. Look at the map on this page. What crops grow in the Southwest today? What do you think the map would look like if no one used irrigation?

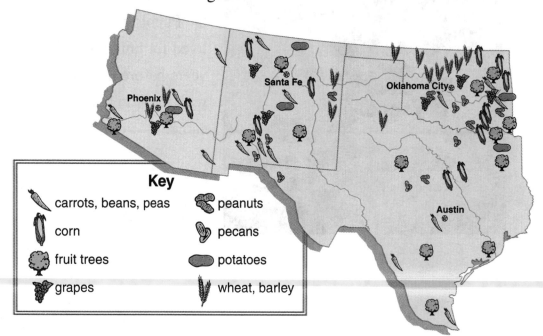

Key

- carrots, beans, peas
- corn
- fruit trees
- grapes
- peanuts
- pecans
- potatoes
- wheat, barley

Spanish Flavors

The Spanish explorers changed the Southwest forever. They brought horses. They brought their own kind of food. They brought a new language. They brought the Roman Catholic religion. They built cities where once there had been open land.

There are many "echoes" of the Spanish settlers in the Southwest today. Many buildings in Southwest cities have a Spanish look. Popular foods like chili con carne came from Spanish cooks. The cattle ranches, so famous for cowboys and roundups, came to be because the early Spanish

A house showing Spanish influence

had let their longhorn cattle run wild. The ranchers rounded up the longhorns and started herds.

The word *ranch* itself comes from the Spanish word *rancho*. When the cattle run wildly in a herd, they *stampede*. That word comes from a Spanish word meaning "crash or uproar." Can you find towns on a map of the Southwest that seem to have Spanish names?

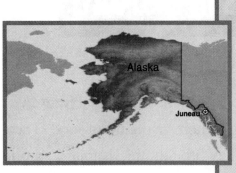

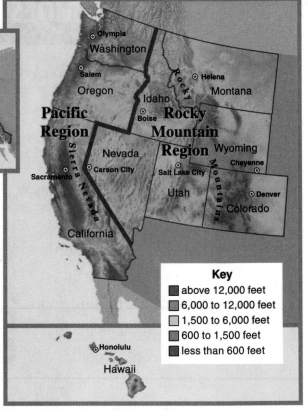

Key
- above 12,000 feet
- 6,000 to 12,000 feet
- 1,500 to 6,000 feet
- 600 to 1,500 feet
- less than 600 feet

The West

The West is made up of two regions: the Rocky Mountain region (Idaho, Montana, Wyoming, Nevada, Utah, and Colorado) and the Pacific region (California, Oregon, Washington, Alaska, and Hawaii). What kept people from settling in the West for many years? The Rocky Mountains were like a giant wall, holding out the growing tide of settlers.

What people lived in the West first? How do you think the white settlers changed the way they lived? They took lands that the Indians had lived on for hundreds of years. They dug it up looking for silver. They built towns and railroads on it. In the end, the Indians lost all their hunting and fishing places.

Many of the states in this region were settled by people in a hurry to find gold and silver. Sutter's Creek was only one of the "rushes" west. What state is Sutter's Creek in? Gold and silver were discovered in Colorado too. Why do you think more people came to Colorado than to California? It was closer to the East.

To Use a Grid Map

1. Get a pencil, a ruler, your textbook, and Notebook page 47.

2. Look at the map of Colorado on your Notebook page. The straight lines down and across the map are helpful for finding places. What do you see on the left and right sides of the grid map? What do you see on the top and bottom edges of the grid map? Use the numbers and letters to find the cities your teacher names.

3. Grid maps come in all sizes. A globe can have a grid drawn on it. Can you find other grid maps in your textbook?

A lot of silver was found in Nevada. Then gold mines brought prospectors, people looking for riches, to Idaho and Oregon. Do you remember who settled Utah and why? Later gold was found in Alaska, and another rush was on.

When the United States bought the territory that is now Alaska, many people thought it was a bad idea. The land seemed too cold and too far away. Today no one thinks that. Alaska, the largest state, has far more than gold. It has many natural resources and vast areas of beautiful wilderness.

Summer beauty in Alaska

Hawaii, the fiftieth state, was not seen by a white man until 1778. Then Captain James Cook sailed into the islands and the Hawaiians greeted him and his crew with food and friendliness. Thirty years later missionaries from New England came to preach the gospel and to build schools and churches.

Island of Hawaii
Summer of 1823

Queen Kapiolani went to the volcano Kilauea, one of the biggest in the world. Many people believed the goddess Pele lived in the volcano and would kill Queen Kapiolani for walking there.

Queen Kapiolani threw stones into the boiling pit of lava. She said, "Jehovah is God. God kindled these fires. I fear not Pele. You must fear and serve God alone."

Those with her sang a hymn and kneeled to pray. The queen's courage helped her people see that her God was the true God.

Keeping Important Objects

Have you ever visited a museum? What was in it? Why do you think people keep things from the past? Sometimes they want to remember a person who owned the objects. Sometimes they want to help people who are born later to know about earlier times. Does your family have special items saved from the past?

John Quincy Adams, the sixth president of the United States, wanted to make a place to keep important things from all over the United States and from all times in our history. And he did. It is called the Smithsonian Institution. It is in Washington, D.C.

The Smithsonian is many museums and study centers together. The National Museum of American History houses the flag that flew over Fort McHenry and inspired the national anthem. It also displays the desk at which Thomas Jefferson sat to write the Declaration of Independence. It even has the first gold nugget found at Sutter's Fort.

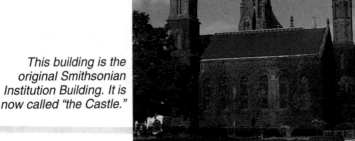

This building is the original Smithsonian Institution Building. It is now called "the Castle."

War Coming!

7

The United States grew a lot in the thirty years after George Washington became the first president. Can you tell from the map something that had changed?

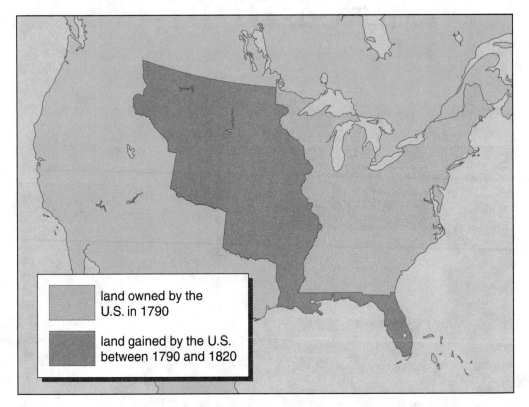

land owned by the U.S. in 1790

land gained by the U.S. between 1790 and 1820

Some other things stayed the same. Many Americans still owned slaves and made them work hard. Some masters treated their slaves well, but many did not. And even a well-treated slave was still a slave. He was not paid or thanked for his work.

Some Americans wanted to stop slavery. Many others did not. "Who will work in our fields?" they asked. Can you remember when Americans first argued about slavery?

The Slavery Question

What almost kept some states from signing the new Constitution? It was slavery. Some states wanted it to go on. Others wanted it stopped. Roger Sherman came up with a plan. It was not exactly what either side wanted. What do you think the men did?

They decided to compromise. They agreed that slave states could bring slaves in for twenty more years. That compromise pleased most of the voters. They signed the Constitution. But the compromise did not solve the problem of slavery.

Some people said that the compromise was "a deal with the devil." Others said that the Constitution gave each state the right to decide about slavery for itself. Years later in the 1820s, the debate over slaves was about to "echo" in another place.

Africans being brought in a ship to the United States to be sold as slaves

When the men who wrote the Constitution made the slavery compromise, they thought they were doing a good thing. They felt sure that slavery would soon end by itself. And it might have, if it had not been for an invention called the *cotton gin.*

Cotton grew well in the warm South. It could be woven into cloth that made comfortable clothing. But the fluffy cotton *bolls* held sticky seeds. Slaves had to remove each seed by hand. Would you like to have that job?

It took too much time and too many slaves to pull the seeds from the cotton. Few people wanted to grow the cotton plants. Then Eli Whitney thought of a way to make removing the seeds easier. His machine could remove the seeds from as much cotton in one day as fifty slaves could by hand.

A typical Southern plantation

The cotton gin made preparing cotton much easier. Many plantation owners wanted to grow cotton now. They could make money from selling the cotton. They bought more farmland and more slaves to tend the cotton plants and run the cotton gin. Cotton soon became the most important crop in the Southern states. People in new territories even began to grow cotton.

Slavery: Yes or No?

Do you remember what a *territory* is? A territory is an area of land that belongs to a country, like the United States. As the United States gained more land in the West, people went to live in these new territories.

People who lived in a territory could not vote for president. They could not choose their own laws. So as soon as they could, people in each territory asked the government to make their territory a state.

Every new state had to answer a very important question: Will this be a free state or a slave state? *Free* meant that slavery would not be allowed there. Look at the map on this page. How many states were free in 1819? How many were slave? The territory of Missouri wanted to be a state. Why do you think Missouri was so important to everyone?

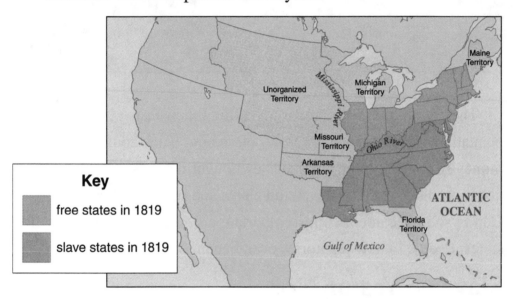

Key

free states in 1819

slave states in 1819

If Missouri became a free state, how many more free states than slave states would there be? People in the North called for Missouri to be a free state. People in the South said it must become a slave state. Everyone argued about it.

Men in Congress yelled at each other. A Southern man said, "If Missouri is not allowed to decide on her own, there are some who would leave the Union." Many states were ready to leave the United States and form their own country.

Henry Clay listened to the yelling. He did not want to see the United States broken up. He came up with the Missouri Compromise. This compromise said that Missouri would be a slave state. But the next state, Maine, would be free.

Congress said that the compromise was good. Maine became a free state in 1820. Missouri became a slave state in 1821. Many people were glad. They hoped that the argument over slavery had been solved.

Thomas Jefferson said that the problem was solved for the moment. "But," he said, "this is not the final sentence." What do you think he meant? Do you think he was right?

Texas

About the time Missouri became a state, people began moving to another new territory. But this territory did not belong to the United States. It belonged to Mexico. Can you find Mexico on the map? It is south of the United States.

When the Mexican ruler said it was all right, the Americans moved to the Texas territory. They built towns and plantations. The hard-working people became citizens of Mexico. They called themselves *Texans*.

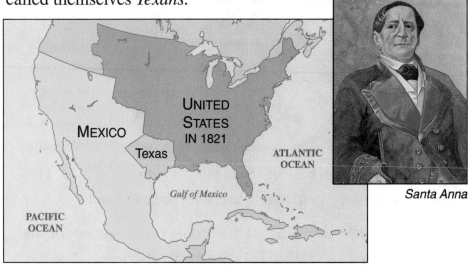

Santa Anna

After about ten years, more Texans than Mexicans lived in the Texas territory. The leaders in Mexico did not like that. They made new laws to keep more Americans from coming to Texas. And the Mexican president, Antonio López de Santa Anna, sent his army to Texas to make sure the Texans obeyed his laws.

Do you think the Texans wanted Santa Anna's army in Texas? "We are tired of obeying strict Mexican laws," they said. "We will be ready to fight." Quickly the men of Texas formed an army of their own.

The Texas army was ready for Santa Anna's men. After just a few battles, the army of Mexico hurried home. The Texans thought that they had won their freedom. But Santa Anna did not agree. He decided to lead his army to Texas. "I will destroy the Texans myself," he said.

The Texans were not ready this time. Most of the men had gone home to their farms and plantations. Only around 180 people stayed in the little town of San Antonio. They were surprised when Santa Anna and several thousand men poured into the town and stopped in front of a mission called the *Alamo.*

Diagram of the Alamo

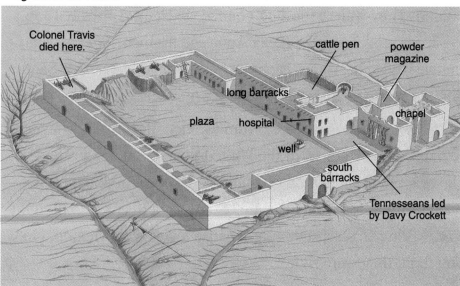

The Texas army gathered together again. But they were not fast enough to save the men in the Alamo. Santa Anna's army killed every man there. Then they burned the farms and houses around the town.

Texans wanted revenge for the deaths of the men in the Alamo. They waited for their chance. Then on April 21, 1836, the Texas army surprised Santa Anna and his men. After a twenty-minute battle, the Texans captured Santa Anna. They made Santa Anna agree to let Texas be a country by itself.

Now that Texas was free from Mexico, the Texans wanted to make their land part of the United States. But Texans had slaves on their big cotton plantations. Do you think the North wanted Texas to become a state? Some Americans also thought that making Texas a state might cause a war with Mexico. Do you think they were right?

War with Mexico

It took almost nine years, but in March of 1845 Texas became a state. How do you think the Mexican leaders felt when they heard the news? They were angry. They still hoped to recapture Texas.

President James K. Polk did not want a war with Mexico. He sent an *ambassador* to talk with the rulers in Mexico. But they would not listen to the ambassador. One year after Texas became a state, the war with Mexico began.

The Mexican War lasted almost two years. Trained soldiers and volunteers fought to keep Texas part of the United States. In the end, the United States won a great deal of land from Mexico. Now the country stretched from one ocean in the East to another ocean in the West.

"Remember the Alamo!" became the battle cry of the Mexican War. This is the front of the Alamo as it looks today.

More Trouble

The end of the Mexican War did not make everyone happy. Before long the North and the South were arguing over the new land. What do you think the arguments were about?

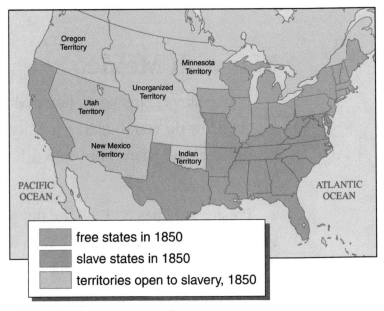

free states in 1850
slave states in 1850
territories open to slavery, 1850

Do you remember what Thomas Jefferson had said? He had said slavery would cause more trouble later. He had been right. In 1850 the territory of California wanted to become a state. How many states were free and how many were slave now? What do you think the problem was?

Henry Clay made another compromise. This time he said that California should be free. But what about other new territories made from the land gained from Mexico? They should be able to decide about slavery for themselves. Mr. Clay also said that all runaway slaves had to be caught and sent back to their masters. What do you think of this compromise?

The compromise passed. But angry people on both sides said that the compromise was not fair. What do you think the people for slavery did not like? What do you think the people against slavery did not like?

No one asked the slaves what they thought. Slaves were not thought of as people. They were called property, like horses. But they were people—with souls, with families, with hopes and fears. More and more slaves were trying to run away. Many were caught and punished. Some made it to freedom.

This slave escaped from Virginia to Pennsylvania inside a wooden box.

Freedom for Slaves

Do you think all people in the North hated slavery? Not everyone did. Some Northerners were afraid that freed slaves would take their jobs. They were glad to help capture runaway slaves. Anyone who caught a runaway got a big reward.

But other people in the North thought they should not return a runaway slave to his master, even if it was the law. They said and believed that owning another human being broke a more important law—God's law. These people wanted to *abolish,* or get rid of, slavery at once. They became known as *abolitionists.*

Harriet Tubman
1820-1913

She had escaped to Pennsylvania. She was free at last. But she was not satisfied. She had to help others escape. And she did. Her people called her "Moses" because she led more than three hundred slaves to the freedom of the North. But not all at one time. She made nineteen daring trips back to slave country.

Harriet Tubman ran part of the escape route known as the *Underground Railroad.* The "railroad" was the back roads and the paths that slaves followed north. The "stations" were houses and barns of people who wanted to help the slaves get away. Harriet was a "conductor." She was fearless and determined.

Her last trip to the South was her most important. She went to get her parents. She dressed like an old woman, walked right into the plantation where she had once been a slave, and took a wagon. Then she got her parents in the wagon and drove them out of slavery forever.

Some abolitionists helped run the Underground Railroad. They hid runaway slaves during the day. At night, they helped the slaves get farther north. What might have happened if they had been caught?

Some abolitionists wrote books and essays. Have you ever heard of *Uncle Tom's Cabin?* That book told about the horrible lives of slaves on a plantation in the South. People all over the country read this story. In the North, more people began to agree with the abolitionists.

Still other abolitionists believed that they could force slave owners to give up their slaves. These abolitionists killed and stole, burned and kidnapped. They thought that it was all right to do hurtful things to reach a good goal. What do you think of their idea? Because this group broke good laws, people in the next new territory lived in danger and fear.

The Right to Choose

What right did Henry Clay's last compromise give to new territories in the Southwest? They could decide for themselves about slavery. The South wanted all territories to be able to choose for themselves. In 1854, the Kansas-Nebraska Act gave two more new territories the right to choose.

Nebraska was too far north to become a slave state. But Kansas was not. People who were for slavery packed up and moved to Kansas. People who were against slavery packed up and moved there too. Why do you think so many people wanted to move to the new territory? Each group wanted to have the most people living in Kansas when it was time to vote.

The people who moved to Kansas were not always peaceful. Each side sent men who would fight to be sure its side won the most votes. The fighters were mean and sneaky. The fighting was so bad that people called the new territory *Bleeding Kansas.*

The right of the people in a new territory to choose about slavery had seemed like a good thing. But with the terrible fighting in Kansas, people began to change their minds. One man was willing to stand up and speak out against the problem. His name was Abraham Lincoln.

A Man Named Lincoln

Abraham Lincoln was not famous. He did not come from a rich family. He was not educated in the finest schools. But his plain and simple way of talking was easy to understand. And many people agreed with what he said.

Abraham Lincoln was born in the woods of Kentucky in 1809. He lived with his family in a one-room log cabin with a dirt floor. In all, he spent about one year in a school. How much more time have you spent in school already? Even though his time in school was short, Abraham did learn to read and write. He taught himself many things by reading books over and over.

Abraham Lincoln was twenty-two when he left home to make a life for himself in Illinois. First he worked as a clerk in a general store. Later he owned his own store. But the store failed, and he found work as a surveyor. He also ran a post office. Would you want to have any of these jobs?

People who met Lincoln knew he was honest and dependable. He was always willing to help wherever he was needed. His friends asked him to run for public office. They wanted him to serve them in the Illinois state congress.

Lincoln's law office was on this street in Springfield. (See the X.)

Lincoln ran and won. He packed up his few belongings and moved to the state capital in Springfield. He worked hard in the congress to make good laws. He studied hard too. Lincoln wanted to become a lawyer. Before long he was one of the best and most trusted lawyers in Springfield.

Abraham Lincoln also wanted to keep slavery out of the new territories. He made speeches about Bleeding Kansas. In one speech he said, "He who would *be* no slave must consent to *have* no slave. Those who deny freedom to others deserve it not for themselves." What do you think about Lincoln's ideas?

Lincoln's ideas made him famous all over the country. About this time, the new Republican Party was formed by abolitionists and others who thought slavery was wrong. This new party picked Lincoln to run for president in 1860.

The South did not want Lincoln to be president. They knew he was against slavery. They thought that he would set all the slaves free. So the Southern states made a plan. If Lincoln won the race for president, they would leave the Union, another name for the United States. They would form a new country.

To Read Circle Graphs

1. Get Notebook page 56, a pencil, and some books, newspapers, or magazines.

2. Circle graphs compare the parts of a whole thing. They show the differences in the sizes of the parts. Listen as your teacher explains the circle graph. Then answer the questions on the Notebook page.

3. Find a circle graph in a book, newspaper, or magazine. How does the graph compare things?

Abraham Lincoln was elected president in 1860. Soon after, South Carolina did what the Southern states had said they would do. It left the Union. Not much later, six more Southern states left the Union. These states made themselves into a new country. They called their new country the Confederate States of America, or the Confederacy.

For more than fifty years, the North and South had argued about slavery. But slavery was not the only thing that made the North and the South different. Most people in the North lived in cities and worked in factories and shops. The Southern people lived and worked on farms or big plantations. Neither side understood the way of life on the other side.

The two sides disagreed, too, on the rights of the states. The South thought that each state could make laws for itself. They

Northern and Southern ways of life differed.

could choose whether to allow slavery or whether to leave the Union. But the North believed that the laws made by the United States were more important than laws made by one state.

By 1860 the problems between the North and the South were too big. A compromise would not work this time. There seemed to be only one way left to settle all the disagreements.

Inside Fort Sumter
Charleston, South Carolina
April 12, 1861

Inside Fort Sumter as it is now

The soldiers in blue coats looked out at Charleston. The city was quiet. The water was quiet. Soon the sun would come up, and soon the soldiers would know what the South planned to do.

Suddenly, a red flash swept across the dark sky. It made an eerie whistle as it went, and sparks shot from it. Then an awful roar, like a thunderclap, shook the fort. A Confederate shell burst over the small group of Union soldiers.

Major Anderson put out his hand to steady himself for the blast. He knew what that shot meant. There was no hope for peace now. The war between North and South had begun.

Fort Sumter after the bombardment

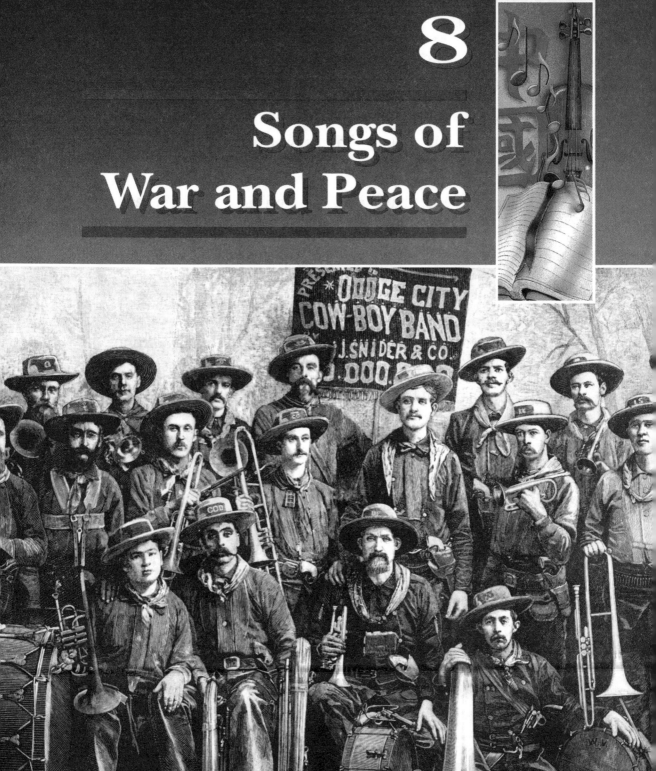

8

Songs of
War and Peace

Do you have a favorite song? Almost everyone does. We like songs with catchy tunes that are fun to sing. We might like one song because it makes us happy and another song because it makes us sad. Some of our favorite songs make us proud to be Americans.

As long as people have lived in America, songwriters here have thought up songs to sing. The songs tell about things that happened to the writers or to people they knew. The songs tell about things that were special to the whole country or to just a small part of it.

We can learn about some important things that happened in the past by learning the songs that were *popular* then. Popular songs are songs that the people loved to hear and sing. Some popular songs from long ago are still loved today. How many of these old-time songs do you already know?

Singing in Times of Peace

Stephen Foster

Many popular songs told about every-day things. One of these songs might tell about home, family, or a favorite pet. It might remind you of someone you love. Stephen Foster wrote this kind of song. He was the first American to make his living by writing songs.

Foster liked music even when he was young. Do you like music? In those days, arts like music and painting were not important to most people. Foster's family hoped he would find something more important to do. But nothing else was important to Foster.

Stephen Foster wrote 189 songs. "Oh, Susanna!" was one of his first. He wrote "Oh, Susanna!" in 1848. The next year, men heading for the gold mines in California made new words for the song. They sang it this way:

Oh, California,
That's the land for me!
I'm bound for San Francisco
With my washbowl on my knee.

Foster's song "Oh, Susanna!" was a favorite of the forty-niners.

Oh, Susanna!

I come from Alabama with my banjo on my knee;
I'm going to Lou'siana, my true love for to see.
It rained all night the day I left,
The weather it was dry;
The sun so hot I froze to death—Susanna, don't you cry.

Chorus:
Oh, Susanna! Oh don't you cry for me;
For I've come from Alabama with my banjo on my knee.

I had a dream the other night when everything was still;
I thought I saw Susanna come a-walking down the hill.
A red, red rose was in her hand,
A tear was in her eye;
I said, "I come from Alabam'. Susanna, don't you cry."

To Read a Line Graph

1. Get Notebook page 58 and a pencil.

2. Line graphs help you see how a thing has changed over time. Each dot on the graph stands for a number. What does the graph on your Notebook page show? What do the numbers across the bottom of the graph represent? What do the numbers on the left side of the graph mean? Answer the questions on the Notebook page.

3. Look back at the circle graph on Notebook page 56. How are a circle graph and a line graph different?

People all over America sang "Oh, Susanna!" But sometimes songs were sung by a smaller group of people. The songs told about things only those people knew. These things were not important to everyone in the country. Can you guess what group of people sang "Git Along, Little Dogies"?

Cowboys sang songs like this one to calm their little dogies. "Little dogies" were the longhorn cattle; each one weighed about one thousand pounds. Do you think the cowboys' name for the cattle was a good one? The job of the cowboys began with the spring roundup. Then they spent most of the spring and summer *driving,* or guiding, the longhorn cattle from the pastureland to the markets. Do you think the cowboys' job sounds like fun?

Many of the songs sung by the cowboys in the West are *folksongs.* We do not know who wrote the words and the music to this kind of song. One person or a group of people might make up a folksong. If others liked the song, they sang it too. But they never wrote it down and tried to sell it as a songwriter would.

Git Along, Little Dogies

As I was a-walkin' one mornin' for pleasure,
I spied a cowpuncher come ridin' along.
His hat was throwed back and his spurs was a-jinglin',
And as he approached he was singin' this song:

Chorus:
Whoopee ti yi yo, git along, little dogies;
It's your misfortune and none of my own.
Whoopee ti yi yo, git along, little dogies;
You know that Montana will be your new home.

Early in springtime we round up the dogies,
Mark 'em and brand 'em and cut off their tails.
Then we all load up the old chuck wagon,
An' hitch up our hosses and start up the trail.

It's whoopin' and yellin' and drivin' the dogies,
And oh how I wish you would only go on!
It's whoopin' and punchin', go on, little dogies;
You know that Montana will be your new home.

Some boys, they go up on the trail just for pleasure,
But that's where they get it most awfully wrong.
You haven't a notion the trouble they give us,
It takes all our time to keep movin' along.

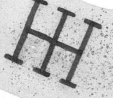

155

Playing Musical Instruments

Do you play a musical instrument? Would you like to learn to play one? It takes practice to play a musical instrument well. People who can play an instrument like the piano or the flute have practiced for a long time.

We can play some instruments by blowing into them. We can play other instruments by tapping or hitting them. A third kind of instrument is played by plucking strings. Which kind do you think would be easiest to play?

The Bible tells about many kinds of musical instruments. David played the harp. The priests in the temple played cymbals and trumpets and harps. Do you know what musical instrument Gideon and his army used? How did all these people use their musical instruments? They used them to bring glory to God.

"Praise him with the sound of the trumpet: praise him with the psaltery and harp.

Praise him with the timbrel and dance: praise him with stringed instruments and organs.

Praise him upon the loud cymbals: praise him upon the high sounding cymbals."

Psalm 150:3-5

Folksongs came from many different groups of people. Some of the folksongs we think of as favorites today came from the slaves. The black people in the South made up songs to help them bear their work and sorrow. "Pick a Bale of Cotton" was one of these songs. Can you guess which slaves sang this one?

Some of these work songs are still popular today. But we remember more a second kind of song the slaves made up. These songs told about people from the Bible. The slaves identified with the hard life of some of the people in these Bible stories. One of their favorite stories was about Moses. God used Moses to lead his people out of slavery. Why do you think slaves liked this story?

We call these slave songs *spirituals*. They tell about the slaves' faith in God to protect and deliver them. Perhaps you know some spirituals. Songs like "Swing Low, Sweet Chariot," "When the Saints Go Marching In," and "Nobody Knows the Trouble I've Seen" are well known. These songs were first sung by groups of slaves who gathered to worship God.

Go Down, Moses

When Israel was in Egypt land,
"Let my people go."
Oppressed so hard they could not stand,
"Let my people go."

Chorus:
Go down, Moses,
Way down in Egypt land,
Tell ol' Pharaoh to let my people go!

"Thus saith the Lord," bold Moses said.
"Let my people go.
If not, I'll strike your first-born dead!
Let my people go."

The Lord told Moses what to do,
"Let my people go,"
To lead the children of Israel through.
"Let my people go."

Lowell Mason
1792-1872

Young Lowell tapped lightly on the door and then entered his friend's shop. George, a little older than Lowell, was bent over an organ. Lowell sat down at a dusty piano in the corner and picked out a tune that he had created. He loved to watch George fix these old organs and pianos, but more than that, he loved music and beautiful songs.

Along with his love of music, Lowell Mason loved the Lord. As he became older, he combined his interest in music with his love for the Lord. By the age of sixteen, Lowell was directing his church choir. A few years later, he wrote his first song. Lowell also directed a band, teaching himself to play different instruments.

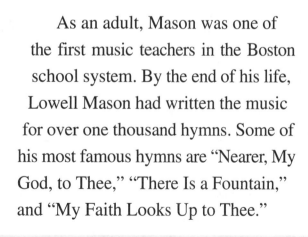

As an adult, Mason was one of the first music teachers in the Boston school system. By the end of his life, Lowell Mason had written the music for over one thousand hymns. Some of his most famous hymns are "Nearer, My God, to Thee," "There Is a Fountain," and "My Faith Looks Up to Thee."

Singing in Wartime

Many songs of America are not light and happy. Songwriters wrote more serious songs when the people wanted them. Patriotic songs told about liberty, freedom, and loyalty to the land. War songs were more serious yet. They called men to fight for their country and their cause. What two groups needed war songs in 1860?

The war song for the South was written in 1859, two years before the war began. Dan Emmett wrote the song on a cold winter weekend. He was a traveling entertainer, and he needed a new song. He remembered how his friends wished to be in the warm South, or Dixie's land, when it was cold outside. Emmett performed the new song on Monday. It was a hit.

Soon people all over the country were singing Emmett's song. The people of the South especially liked the song. It made them proud of their Southern land. When Confederate soldiers found that it was easy to march to, "Dixie" became their favorite song. Dan Emmett was a Northerner, loyal to the Union. How do you think he felt when his song became so important to the Confederacy?

Dixie

I wish I was in the land of cotton,
Old times there are not forgotten,
Look away! Look away! Look away! Dixie Land.
In Dixie Land where I was born in,
Early on one frosty mornin',
Look away! Look away! Look away! Dixie Land.

Chorus:
Then I wish I was in Dixie,
Hooray! Hooray!
In Dixie Land, I'll take my stand to live and die in Dixie;
Away, away, away down south in Dixie,
Away, away, away down south in Dixie.

There's buckwheat cakes and cornbread batter,
Makes you fat or a little fatter;
Look away! Look away! Look away! Dixie Land.
Then hoe it down and scratch your gravel,
To Dixie's Land I'm bound to travel,
Look away! Look away! Look away! Dixie Land.

To Make a Musical Instrument

1. Gather one of the following sets of materials.
   a. an empty coffee can or an oatmeal canister, a piece of vinyl or cloth to cover the opening, and string or a rubber band
   b. tape, poster board, and a mouthpiece from a brass instrument, if possible

2. Use the first set of materials to make a drum. Stretch the vinyl tightly over the opening of the can. Fasten it in place by wrapping it with the rubber band or string. Tap the vinyl with your hand or the end of your pencil. How does it sound?

3. Make a bugle using the second set of materials. Shape the poster board into a cone and tape or staple the seam. If you have a mouthpiece from a brass instrument, place the mouthpiece into the smaller end of the cone. Blow into the mouthpiece or the small end of the cone. How does your instrument sound?

4. The Union and Confederate armies used the drum and the bugle. What do you think they used them for? How can you find out?

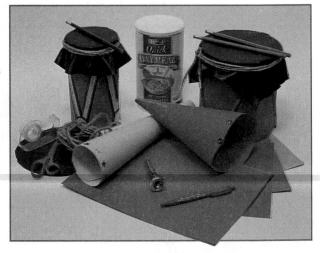

The song that most people think of as the war song of the North was not even written when the war began. That is, the words were not written. The tune had been around for a long time. At the beginning of the American Civil War, soldiers sang "John Brown's Body" to the tune. The song was about a man some people in the North thought was a hero. But the words of the song did not fit the tune.

Julia Ward Howe heard Union soldiers singing "John Brown's Body." A friend said, "That tune needs better words. Julia, you should write new words for it." She promised to try. That night as she listened to more soldiers tramp past her window, she thought of new words. And she quickly wrote them down on a scrap of paper. Soon Union soldiers everywhere were singing Howe's words to the old tune.

As the years went by, the things people sang about changed. But people sang some of the old favorites over and over again. The old favorite songs are national songs because they are part of America's heritage. Today people may not know the stories of the national songs. But they know when a song makes them happy or when a song moves them to love and serve God better. These are the songs America loves to sing.

The Battle Hymn of the Republic

Mine eyes have seen the glory of the coming of the Lord;
He is trampling out the vintage where the grapes of wrath
 are stored;
He hath loosed the fateful lightning of his terrible swift sword;
His truth is marching on.

Chorus:

Glory, glory, hallelujah!
Glory, glory, hallelujah!
Glory, glory, hallelujah!
His truth is marching on.

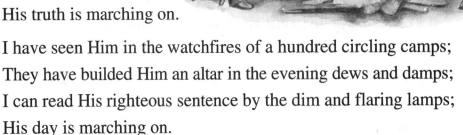

I have seen Him in the watchfires of a hundred circling camps;
They have builded Him an altar in the evening dews and damps;
I can read His righteous sentence by the dim and flaring lamps;
His day is marching on.

He has sounded forth the trumpet that shall never sound retreat;
He is sifting out the hearts of men before His judgment seat.
O be swift, my soul, to answer Him! Be jubilant, my feet!
Our God is marching on.

In the beauty of the lilies Christ was born across the sea,
With a glory in His bosom that transfigures you and me;
As He died to make men holy, let us die to make men free,
While God is marching on.

164

9
North
Against South

The firing at Fort Sumter did not kill one soldier on either side. The city of Charleston was not damaged at all. Most of the people in the United States thought the whole war would be over in three months.

It was more than three months, though, before the first big battle of the Civil War even began. President Abraham Lincoln had called for seventy-five thousand volunteers to help fight for the North. The men had come. They were training for war.

Look at the chart. Did the Confederacy or the Union have more free people? Who had more miles of railroad? Which side had more factories? Who produced more firearms? Why do you think the Union thought the Confederacy could be beaten quickly?

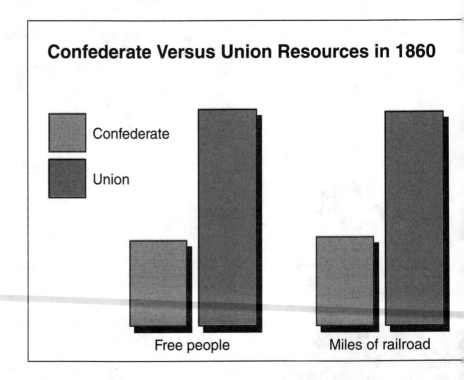

Confederate Versus Union Resources in 1860

Confederate

Union

Free people

Miles of railroad

The Union had many advantages. It had more men. It had more factories to make things an army would need. What things might these factories make? And the Union had more ways to move the soldiers and the supplies to the places that needed them. Why do you think this was important?

But the Confederate States had some advantages too. Some of the best military leaders were from the South. Do you think these men stayed in the United States Army when their states left the Union? They did not. They left the Union army to become leaders in the Confederate army.

These leaders knew that something else would help their side. To make the Confederate States part of the United States again, the Union army would have to *invade*. That means the Union would have to send its army onto Confederate land. It would need more men and more supplies to invade than the Confederate army would need to protect the Southern land.

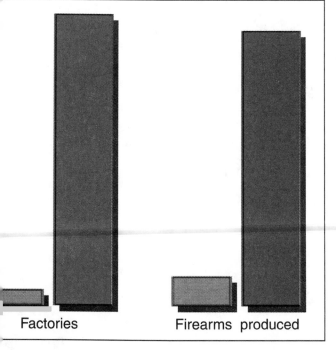

Factories   Firearms produced

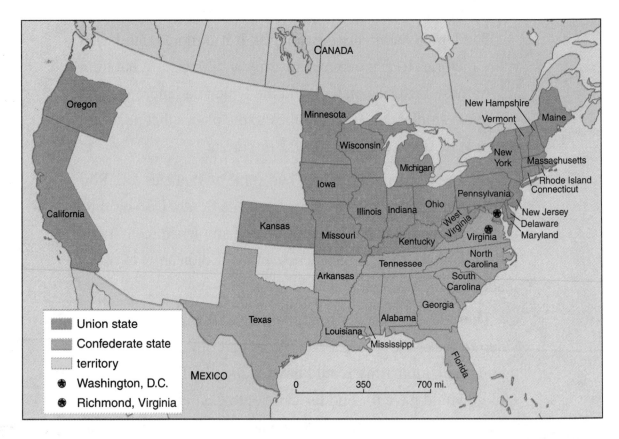

This is how a map of the country looked in May 1861. Eleven states had left the Union and joined the Confederate States of America. How many states were still part of the Union?

The leaders in the new Confederacy finally decided the city of Richmond would be their *capital.* The capital of a country is the home of the president and other leaders. It is where they work to make the laws. Can you find the Union capital?

Keeping Journals

Much of what modern people know about the American Civil War comes from journals. Journals of soldiers, journals of wives who waited at home, journals of freed slaves, and journals of preachers. From those pages we learn what life was like in Lincoln's day. One soldier wrote:

We are in a field...on the side of a hill, near the top... A blanket spread on the ground is our bed, while another spread over us is our covering. A narrow strip of muslin, drawn over a pole about three feet from the ground, open at the both ends, the wind and the rain... beating in upon us,...and creeping things crawling over us, and... great hungry mosquitoes biting every uncovered inch of us... We each got a piece

A Southern wife tells of different hardships: "In the street a barrel of flour sells for one hundred and fifty dollars. . . . Mrs. Davis says . . . they are going to dispense with their carriage and horses."

Do you keep a journal? What does it tell of your times? Why do you think fewer people keep journals now?

The First Big Battle

The soldiers in both armies listened and learned; then they *drilled,* or practiced, again and again. Most of the soldiers were *volunteers,* men who had offered to fight for their countries. The volunteers had never fought in a battle before.

The people at home became impatient. This drilling was taking too long. Do you think the soldiers needed much practice? They did, but the people wanted the fighting to begin soon. The sooner it began, the sooner it would be over, they thought.

The generals, or leaders, on both sides listened to the people. They told the soldiers to be ready for battle. Then Union General McDowell marched his men into Virginia. Was Virginia a Confederate state or a Union state?

General McDowell and his army headed to the South. They wanted to capture Manassas Junction. It was a place in which two railroads met. One railroad led to Washington, D.C. What was important about that city? If McDowell could capture that spot, he could protect the Union capital.

People from Washington followed the Union army. They rode in fancy carriages wearing their Sunday best. They brought picnic lunches to eat while they watched the battle. Do you think that was a wise thing to do?

The Union army and the Confederate army met on the banks of a creek called Bull Run. The creek was near Manassas Junction. The fighting began early in the morning and went on for most of the day. In the end, the Union soldiers turned and ran. They ran past the people with the fancy carriages and picnic lunches. Some soldiers ran all the way back to Washington, D.C.

Thomas J. "Stonewall" Jackson
1824-63

At one point during the Battle of Bull Run, the Union seemed to be winning. The Confederate generals were afraid their men would turn and run. One man saw brave and calm General Thomas Jackson leading his troops. The man called out, "Look! There stands Jackson like a stone wall. Rally behind the Virginians!" After the battle everyone called General Jackson by a new name—Stonewall Jackson.

Thomas Jackson's father and mother died when he was very young. Then Tom lived with his uncle. He liked to help with the work on the big plantation. Tom worked hard at everything he did. When he was older, he got the chance to go to a special school called West Point. Do you think he worked hard there too? He learned how to be a good soldier.

Jackson also worked hard for the Lord. He started a Sunday school for the slaves where he lived. During the war, he tried to keep from fighting on a Sunday. If he did have to do battle on the Lord's Day, he set aside another day in the week to worship God. Jackson praised God every time he won a battle.

Stonewall Jackson died before the war ended. His own men shot him accidentally. His soldiers and everyone in the South mourned. They had lost one of their best generals.

The Union and the Confederate soldiers learned important lessons at the Battle of Bull Run. Both sides knew now that the war would not be over in just a few months. Each knew the enemy would fight hard for its country. It would be a long, bloody war.

Both armies also learned something about needing uniforms. The Union soldiers, or *Yankees,* were supposed to wear blue. The Confederate soldiers were supposed to wear gray. But before this battle, neither army had a uniform. The soldiers wore whatever clothes they had. Why might this be a problem?

During the battle a group of soldiers dressed in blue came upon some Union soldiers. Who do you think the soldiers in blue were? The Union men thought they were more Union soldiers coming to help. But the soldiers in blue were Confederates. They did not plan to help the Union soldiers. The Confederates shot and captured almost four hundred Union men.

New Leaders for the Armies

President Lincoln learned something from the battle too. He saw that General McDowell was not a good leader for the Union army. He picked General George McClellan to be the army's new leader. The president had a good reason for picking General McClellan. He had won small battles in the West. Maybe he could win bigger battles too.

General McClellan was a planner. He planned what he should do with the Union army. He planned how the men would be trained. Then he made sure that their training went as he had planned. After many months the general had 150,000 men who were ready to fight.

But while General McClellan worked with the army, President Lincoln grew tired of waiting. He thought that McClellan might never do more than drill and practice with the men. Finally the president told McClellan that he must lead the men into a battle.

McClellan alone and with some of his men

Spying from Balloons

One day near the beginning of the war, the Southern soldiers saw an amazing sight: a colorful flying ball in the sky over their camp. In a basket under it was a Northern soldier, looking down on them. The Grays tried to shoot the thing down, but it landed safely on the ground.

Soon a dazzling silk balloon was spying over the Blues' tents. Up and up it flew, dragging ropes behind. The Blues tried to catch the ropes to pull the bright balloon down. They could not. But it came down on its own far away. And the best-trained balloonist of the South was glad to be on the ground again.

Another Southern general wanted a balloon to spy with too. Women from many Southern towns sent their best silk ball gowns to the army. What did the soldiers need with ball gowns? They needed the light material to make a balloon. But the South never used this balloon to spy on the Blues. The Union soldiers captured it before it ever left the ground.

General McClellan moved his huge army. He planned to attack the city of Richmond. Do you remember why Richmond was important? McClellan was a good planner, but he was not a good leader in battle. The men in blue lost many battles. The Confederates pushed them back to where they had started.

By now the Confederate army had a new leader too. General Robert E. Lee took charge of the Grays after the first leader was shot. Of all the good generals in the South, Robert E. Lee was one of the best. Lee had worked with many leaders of the Union army. He knew how they acted in battle. And he made good guesses when he did not know.

Now the new leader of the Confederate army decided to take the war into the North. Lee thought he might scare the people there into giving up on the war. He headed his men toward Pennsylvania.

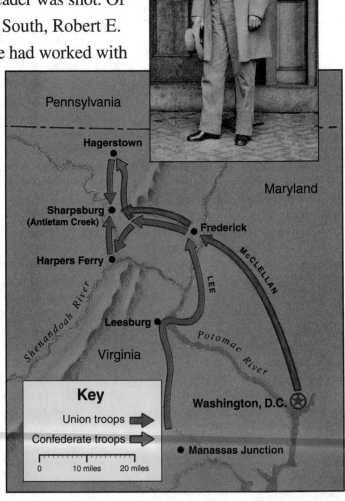

Robert E. Lee

Pennsylvania

Hagerstown

Maryland

Sharpsburg
(Antietam Creek)

Frederick

McCLELLAN

Harpers Ferry

LEE

Shenandoah River

Leesburg

Virginia

Potomac River

Key

Union troops

Confederate troops

Washington, D.C.

Manassas Junction

0   10 miles   20 miles

Freedom at Last

Since the beginning of the war, some people had been asking the president to free the slaves in the South. Lincoln and the other Union leaders said, "We are fighting this war to keep the states together. The war is not about freeing the slaves. We will do something about them later." But the abolitionists kept asking Lincoln to do something soon.

Finally the president agreed. He understood that freeing the slaves would hurt the South. It might even help the North win the war. But Lincoln did not want to make his announcement about freeing the slaves right away. He decided to wait until the Union army won a battle.

The Blues did not have to wait long for another chance to win a battle. President Lincoln heard that General Lee was marching his army into the North. He sent General McClellan to catch him. This time the two armies met on the banks of Antietam Creek near the little village of Sharpsburg, Maryland.

The Antietam battlefield today

177

Mathew Brady
1823-96

The smoke had not yet cleared from the battlefield. But Mr. Brady was out there, setting up his huge camera, calling for the glass plates to put into it. He had been the richest photographer in New York. Now he was quickly becoming poor.

Mathew Brady felt a duty to photograph the worst war his country—or the world—had ever seen. But the government told him he had to pay his own way. By the end of the war, Brady had taken thirty-five hundred photos and had spent all of his one hundred thousand dollars in savings.

Mathew Brady

Brady worked hard the rest of his life and paid off his debts. But he never had much money again. When he died, he left only a cane and a ring. But the United States had a priceless treasure: thousands of pictures of men and women who shaped history.

Two of the many photographs taken by Mathew Brady

The fighting was fierce. It was the worst single day in all the war. When it was over, both armies knew that neither had really won the battle. But the men in gray went back to the South. Their invasion had failed.

President Lincoln's first reading of the Emancipation Proclamation before the cabinet

Now President Lincoln felt that it was time to make his announcement. Just days after the battle, the president read the *Emancipation Proclamation.* Can you guess what *emancipation* means? It means "freeing." Lincoln's announcement said that slaves in states outside the Union were "forever free."

The president gave the Confederate States a little time to think about his announcement. If the states came back into the Union before January 1, 1863, the people could keep their slaves. Do you think any states came back? None did. The war went on.

The Union Hotel Hospital
Washington, D.C.
Mid-December 1862

Before the American Civil War, almost all nurses were men. But with so many men needed in the armies, women volunteered to help. More than three thousand women became nurses during the war.

Army hospitals were often dirty and crowded. The Union Hotel Hospital was one of the worst. It was cold and damp and dark. Sickening smells filled the rooms and hallways.

Many of the patients had been wounded in battles. But other patients were sick with diseases like pneumonia and measles. A nurse's day was filled with washing faces, passing out medicine, and feeding the men. If the nurse had time, she would read to the men or help them to write letters to home. Sometimes she had to comfort the family of a dead soldier.

Since the beginning of the war, slaves had come to the camps of the Union army. The Union soldiers called these slaves *contraband* of war. Contraband is property taken from the enemy. Why were the slaves called contraband?

The Emancipation Proclamation made a change in the way the Union leaders thought. The slaves were no longer contraband but free men and women. The Union army gave jobs to the freed slaves. Some washed clothes and cooked for the soldiers. Others helped to dig ditches and care for the horses that belonged to the army. Soon there were more freed slaves than there were jobs for them to do. What do you think the Union leaders did then?

The Union leaders formed *regiments,* or groups, of black soldiers. The men got uniforms and guns. They learned how to march and shoot. Many freed slaves signed up to fight. Free black men from the North volunteered too. Most of the officers of these regiments were white men. But Major Martin R. Delany was the first black officer in the Union army.

Martin R. Delany

Gettysburg

It was almost a year before the Confederate army tried to invade the North again. General Lee's first try had not worked. But he still believed that he could scare the North into ending the war. He just needed to win a battle on Union land. So he headed his army toward Pennsylvania again.

The Union army followed Lee and his men. They marched north, neither army knowing exactly where the other army was. Men from the Union and Confederate armies ran into each other near the little town of Gettysburg. The meeting was not what either army had planned. But now the battle would be fought here.

Lee's army meets Northern troops north and west of Gettysburg, driving them through town. Union forces rally on Cemetery Ridge and Culp's Hill. In the meantime, Union reinforcements are arriving throughout the night.

The Confederates attack the left and right flanks, almost succeeding. Union troops hold Culp's Hill and Little Round Top.

After a two-hour artillery barrage by 140 guns, 15,000 Confederates march toward the Union center. "Pickett's Charge" fails. Lee's forces withdraw on July 4, returning to Virginia.

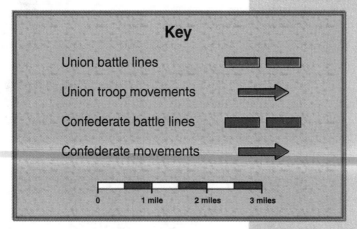

Key

Union battle lines

Union troop movements

Confederate battle lines

Confederate movements

0   1 mile   2 miles   3 miles

To Read a Picture Map

1. You will need the map on pages 182-83 of your textbook.

2. Look at the picture map. What does the map show? What things tell us that the picture is a map?

3. Find the place called Devil's Den. What place is north of Devil's Den? Find Cemetery Ridge. What army fought from the top of the ridge? Answer other questions your teacher asks. Then study the map and make up questions of your own.

4. Compare the picture map with the map on page 176. How are the maps different? How are they the same?

The Battle of Gettysburg is one of the most famous battles of the American Civil War. Can you guess why? More men were hurt or killed at Gettysburg than during any other battle. The fighting lasted three days. Then the beaten Grays went south again. Their army was never quite so strong again.

When the fighting was over, the whole town of Gettysburg became a hospital. Wounded men were carried to homes and churches and barns. Many townspeople kept busy caring for the soldiers. But others helped in a different way. They buried the more than six thousand soldiers who died.

Gettysburg National Cemetery

The people of Gettysburg wanted a special place to bury these men. They bought land on Cemetery Hill. Can you find Cemetery Hill on the picture map? They made the land into a National Soldiers Cemetery. When the cemetery was ready, many people came to see it. They listened to President Lincoln speak about the brave soldiers who had fought for their beliefs.

The End, at Last

When the soldiers fought at Gettysburg, the American Civil War was more than two years old. In the North and South, families were ready for the fighting to end. They wanted their sons and husbands and fathers to come home. But it would take almost two more years for the end of the war to come. And it would take another new leader for the Union army.

The Union army had many different leaders. President Lincoln had not yet found a leader as good as the South's General Lee. But he believed that his new choice would be the man to win the war.

Ulysses S. Grant

Ulysses S. Grant was a strong leader. He had already won battles for the Union in the West. The army he led had taken Forts Donelson and Henry. Then his forces had won at Vicksburg and Chattanooga. General Grant knew how to fight. And he would not give up until the Union had won the war.

General Grant pushed his army against General Lee's men. Sometimes fighting went on for days at a time. Even when it seemed that he had lost the battle, Grant would not turn back. General Lee had thought faster and moved quicker than the other Union leaders. But he could not outdo General Grant.

Finally the Confederate army and people could take no more. And General Robert E. Lee knew that his army could not win. His men were tired and hungry. Many were barefoot and dressed in rags. About half his men did not even have guns anymore. General Lee decided to surrender. Do you think he made a wise decision?

Both North and South were glad that the long and bloody war was over. The Union and the Confederacy were one country again. President Lincoln wanted to "bind up the wounds" of bitterness and pain felt by all Americans.

Richmond, Virginia, in 1865

Sunday, April 9, 1865
Afternoon

Appomattox Court House, Virginia

The horses of General Lee and General Grant stood quietly outside a farmhouse near the last battlefield of the war. Men also stood quietly around, hardly talking. Inside the house, the two generals were deciding how the war would finally end.

Grant and Lee sat at small tables. Their aides stood along the walls. Grant said, "I will write out the terms." Lee nodded. When Grant finished, Lee read the paper. He thanked Grant for letting his men keep their own horses. Then Colonel Parker, an Iroquois in the Northern army, copied the paper. Both generals signed it. Grant then told one of his men to see that food was sent to the whole Southern army.

Lee and Grant stood and shook hands. Then Lee swung into his saddle and rode away, his gray uniform straight, his hair shining white. Along the fences, his men cheered for him. One soldier called out, "We love you just as well as ever, General Lee."

McClean House at Appomattox Court House, Virginia, where the surrender took place

The Thirteenth Amendment

Amendment XIII: *Slavery*

Section 1. Neither slavery nor involuntary servitude, except as punishment for crime whereof the party shall have been duly convicted, shall exist within the United States, or any place subject to their jurisdiction.

Section 2. Congress shall have power to enforce this article by appropriate legislation.

The Emancipation Proclamation had freed the slaves in the Confederate States. But slavery still went on in territories and some other places. Some people wished that the writers of the Constitution had done away with slavery from the start. Others said that the Constitution needed an amendment. *Amendments* are additions to the Constitution. What do you think it means to amend something?

The amendment about slavery said that no slaves could be held anywhere in the United States or in any of its lands. How is this amendment different from the Emancipation Proclamation? The Congress did not pass the amendment at first.

President Lincoln said that it was "only a question of time" until the amendment would pass. "May we not agree," he asked the Congress, "that the sooner the better?" In 1865 the amendment passed and slavery ended, though the wrongs "echo" in our land to this day.

President Lincoln never got to see his nation restored. Just six days after the end of the fighting, a Southern man named John Wilkes Booth shot the president. He thought what he did would help the South. Instead he took away the South's best hope for peaceful reunion with the North.

Four years of war had left an ugly mark on the South. It took time and hard work to make new homes and farms and factories. Slowly the South rebuilt. But it was many, many years before the anger and bad feelings of the Civil War began to heal.

John Wilkes Booth

SURRAT.   BOOTH.   HAROLD.

War Department, Washington, April 20, 1865,

$100,000 REWARD!

THE MURDERER

Of our late beloved President, Abraham Lincoln,

IS STILL AT LARGE.

$50,000 REWARD

Will be paid by this Department for his apprehension, in addition to any reward offered by Municipal Authorities or State Executives.

$25,000 REWARD

Will be paid for the apprehension of JOHN H. SURRATT, one of Booth's Accomplices.

$25,000 REWARD

Will be paid for the apprehension of David C. Harold, another of Booth's accomplices.

LIBERAL REWARDS will be paid for any information that shall conduce to the arrest of either of the above-named criminals, or their accomplices.

All persons harboring or secreting the said persons, or either of them, or aiding or assisting their concealment or escape, will be treated as accomplices in the murder of the President and the attempted assassination of the Secretary of State, and shall be subject to trial before a Military Commission and the punishment of DEATH.

Let the stain of innocent blood be removed from the land by the arrest and punishment of the murderers.

All good citizens are exhorted to aid public justice on this occasion. Every man should consider his own conscience charged with this solemn duty, and rest neither night nor day until it be accomplished.

EDWIN M. STANTON, Secretary of War.

DESCRIPTIONS.—BOOTH is Five Feet 7 or 8 inches high, slender build, high forehead, black hair, black eyes, and wears a heavy black moustache.

JOHN H. SURRAT is about 5 feet, 9 inches. Hair rather thin and dark; eyes rather light; no beard. Would weigh 145 or 150 pounds. Complexion rather pale and clear, with color in his cheeks. Wore light clothes of fine quality. Shoulders square; chest broad rather prominent; chin narrow; ears projecting at the top; forehead rather low and square, but broad. Parts his hair on the right side; neck rather long. His lips are firmly set. A Man neat.

DAVID C. HAROLD is five feet six inches high, hair dark, eyes dark, eyebrows rather heavy, full face, nose short, hand short and fleshy, feet small, instep high, round bodied, naturally quick and active, slightly closes his eyes when looking at a person.

NOTICE—In addition to the above, State and other authorities have offered rewards amounting to almost one hundred thousand dollars, making an aggregate of about TWO HUNDRED THOUSAND DOLLARS.

Reward poster printed after the death of President Lincoln

"If my people, which are called by my name, shall humble themselves, and pray, and seek my face, and turn from their wicked ways; then will I hear from heaven, and will forgive their sin, and will heal their land."

II Chronicles 7:14

10
America
Celebrates

"Happy birthday to you. Happy birthday to you. Happy birthday, dear. . . . Happy birthday to you!"

Every person has a birthday, and most people like to have others help them *celebrate* their birthdays. To celebrate means to set apart a special time for remembering and for having fun. What kind of things do you do to celebrate your birthday?

Birthdays are not the only special days for celebrating. Can you think of other days that you celebrate? In America there are many days for celebrating. We call those days *holidays*. Your family and friends celebrate your birthday. But everyone, all across the country, celebrates holidays.

Famous Birthday Celebrations

Sometimes a birthday celebration can become a holiday. When George Washington was president, people celebrated his birthday, February 22, 1732. (When he was a general, the men in the American army also celebrated his birthday. They could not give him a big party. But they played songs for him and wished him a happy day.) In Philadelphia, men fired cannons and rang church bells. Everyone wanted to shake George Washington's hand and wish him a happy day.

Americans still celebrate George Washington's birthday. They remember him because of the things he did. He led the American army during the War for Independence. He helped to write the Constitution. He became the country's first president. On February 22, Americans think about the man they call the Father of Our Country.

George Washington

Abraham Lincoln

Americans celebrate a second birthday in February. Abraham Lincoln was born February 12, 1809. His family did not have much money. And there was little time for Abe to go to school. Life was hard in the backwoods where Abe lived.

Young Abe Lincoln did not seem to have much going for him. But he studied hard and worked hard. He kept his promises. And he became one of the best presidents America has ever had. He was a strong and brave and wise leader during the terrible Civil War. He helped to bring America back together.

Today in most places, Americans celebrate the birthdays of these two presidents on one day. Presidents' Day is the third Monday in February. On that day, they honor two men who helped to make their country free for everyone.

Building Monuments

One way to help people remember an important person is to name a holiday for him. But it is not the only way. People sometimes build a *monument* to help people remember. Have you ever seen a monument?

A monument is a building or a statue. Usually, an artist or a builder makes the monument from stone. He puts the monument where people can see it. When people visit the monument, they remember the person it honors. Sometimes we call a monument a *memorial.* What smaller word can you hear in the word "memorial"?

Many cities have monuments. Two of America's best-known monuments were built to remind us of presidents. You can see the Washington Monument and the Lincoln Memorial in the same city. Do you know the name of that city? The city is Washington, D.C. It is America's capital.

Washington Monument

Lincoln Memorial

Easter

Each spring we celebrate a special holiday. On this day, we honor a person who was not a president. He was someone far more important. We remember the most important thing He did. Do you know what we remember at *Easter?*

"And the angel answered and said unto the women, Fear not ye: for I know that ye seek Jesus, which was crucified. He is not here: for he is risen, as he said, Come, see the place where the Lord lay."

Matthew 28:5-6

We remember the Savior, Jesus Christ. We think about how He died on the cross to save all men from sin. We are joyful when we remember that He rose from the dead. Because He died for our sins and rose again, we can live forever with Him in heaven.

Memorial Day

Memorial Day is another springtime holiday. Each year on May 30, Americans think about the men and women who died in wars. They think about how these soldiers fought to make America great. Many people put flowers and flags on the graves of those brave men and women. The flowers and flags remind us that people gave their lives to make America free.

Americans celebrated the first Memorial Day a few years after the Civil War ended. No one knows for sure who first thought of this holiday. But it was called "Decoration Day" then. Why do you think the people called it that?

Flag Day

You may see America's flag each day. You may even have one in your classroom. But on one day of the year you will see the flag in many other places too. The flag flies at homes and businesses on that day. Many Americans display the flag on June 14. That is the flag's "birthday."

What do you think of when you look at the flag? Each part of the flag means something. The thirteen stripes make us think of the thirteen colonies. Those colonies fought for their freedom. They became the United States of America. How many stars does the American flag have? There are fifty stars—one for each state in the United States today.

Even the colors have special meanings. Red stands for courage. It makes us think of the men who fought to make America great. It reminds us to have courage to do what is right. White in the stripes and the stars stands for liberty. Liberty means freedom from unwanted rulers. And blue stands for loyalty. It reminds us of the men and women who cared more for their country than they did for themselves.

To Fold the Flag

1. Get an American flag. (You may want a beach towel to practice with first.) Work with your Heritage Studies partner.

2. Open the flag out flat. You hold the striped end while your friend holds the end with the stars. Be sure that the flag does not touch the floor.

3. Fold the flag in half the long way; then fold it in half again. Fold your end up to the right side, making a triangle. Continue folding the triangle shape.

4. Tuck the end of the flag in as your teacher shows you. This will keep the flag folded. What does the folded flag look like? Do you know any rules for taking care of the flag?

Independence Day

Independence Day is a holiday with two names. We know it as the Fourth of July too. It is America's birthday. On that day Americans remember how their country began.

Fifty-six men met in Philadelphia. They came from every colony in America. These men knew that the people of the colonies were tired of King George's rules. They had asked him before to make better laws. Do you remember what King George did instead?

The men voted. They decided to tell the world that the colonies did not belong to the king. The men said the people in America were part of a new country. Today the United States of America is a great country. Americans celebrate their freedom with parades, picnics, and fireworks.

Fireworks over Washington, D.C.

To Plan a Parade

1. Gather some construction paper, crepe paper, tape, paint, paintbrushes, and clothes for costumes. Also find some wood blocks, cardboard boxes, tin cans, and wagons.

2. First, make a list on the chalkboard of things you might see in a parade. Include as many things as you can think of. Then decide which ones you will want for your parade. Which one will come first in the parade? What will be last?

3. Choose a day and a time for your parade. What will you celebrate with the parade? Invite other people to watch.

4. Divide the work among the people who will be in the parade. Let each person make an instrument or put together a costume or decorate a "float." Plan your work so that everything will be finished by the day of the parade.

Columbus Day

Three little ships sailed west from the country of Spain. The men on the ships were afraid. Do you know why? They were sure the world was flat. They thought that their ships might sail off the edge of the world.

Their leader was not frightened. Christopher Columbus believed that the earth was like a ball. He thought he could find Asia by sailing west. His plan would give the people in Spain an easy way to get things like silk, pepper, and cinnamon from Asia.

Today we know that Columbus was both right and wrong. The world is like a ball, just as he said. But the land Columbus found was not Asia; it was a "new" part of the world. People in North America and South America celebrate Columbus Day on October 12. They remember the day that Columbus found a "new" land.

Near San Salvador
October 12, 1492

Three ships waited close to an island. Christopher Columbus and some of his men sailed in smaller boats toward the shore.

The island people watched from the shore. They had seen the large boats with white sails far out to sea. They had thought the boats were three white birds.

At first the island people, or *Arawaks,* were afraid. Then they saw Columbus and his men. The Arawaks brought the white men gifts. They thought the white men were gods.

Christopher Columbus believed that he was on an island near India. He called the island people *Indians.*

Thanksgiving

Pilgrims, Indians, harvest, feast. What do these words make you think of? They remind us of Thanksgiving, of course. Almost four hundred years ago, the Separatists and other Pilgrims made a special feast. They asked their friends the Indians to join them. Did the Indians come? They did, and they brought even more food. The feast lasted for three days.

Why did the Pilgrims prepare such a big feast? They had lived through a cold winter without much to eat. They had worked hard in the spring to plant food. The Indians told them the things to grow. Now they had enough food to eat during the next cold winter. The Pilgrims wanted to thank God for His love and care for them. They wanted to thank Him, too, for bringing them to a new home in which they could worship Him.

Our Thanksgiving is a family holiday. Some people travel many miles to be with their parents, grandparents, and others they love. They gather to thank the Lord for the good things He has given them. And they remember the brave Pilgrims and their Indian friends.

Christmas

One of the last holidays of the year is a favorite one for many people. It reminds us of the birth of Jesus. Do you know the name of this holiday?

We celebrate Christmas at the end of December. Long ago, people decided to celebrate Jesus' birth on December 25. Do you think they knew when Jesus' birthday was? They did not. We do not know either. But we still celebrate His birth on the day they chose.

Many people decorate and give gifts at Christmas.

People today think of Christmas in many ways. Some people think of it as a time to give and get gifts. Others think of it as a time to do good things for those they love. And a few people think of it as a time for parties and pretty decorations. All of these happy things are part of our celebrations. But they are not the most important part. We know that remembering God's gift, Jesus, is what makes Christmas special.

Why do we celebrate so many holidays? Holidays help us remember things that happened long ago. We like to think about brave things people did. Americans want to learn about what their country was like in the past. And most of all we need to be reminded of the things God has given His people—a good country, His Son, and a home in heaven.

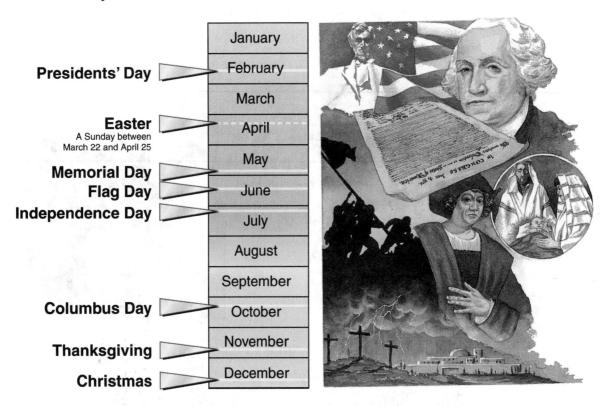

	January
Presidents' Day	February
	March
Easter A Sunday between March 22 and April 25	April
	May
Memorial Day **Flag Day**	June
Independence Day	July
	August
	September
Columbus Day	October
Thanksgiving	November
Christmas	December

"Remember the days of old, consider the years of many generations: ask thy father, and he will shew thee; thy elders, and they will tell thee."

Deuteronomy 32:7

11
Railroads

The huge black monster puffed and chugged across the prairie. It breathed out smoke—sometimes grayish white, other times thick black and full of sparks—as it rolled along. People and animals rushed to get out of the path of the giant beast. But other people followed close behind the monster in a long line. They calmly read, ate, talked, and even slept. What was this monster, and where was it leading those people?

The big black contraption was not really a monster, but for a time, some people thought of it as one. It was a *locomotive,* and it pulled a *train* of cars. Trains like this one were a new way of traveling from place to place.

Early Ways to Travel

Before the early 1800s, people traveled in one of three ways. Can you name these ways? The easiest way to travel was by boat. Boats traveled across oceans and down rivers, canals, and streams. But boat travel was not very handy. People could not always get to where they wanted to go when they traveled by boats. Rivers, canals, and oceans did not go everywhere. What other ways did people travel?

> *"We took sweet counsel together, and walked unto the house of God in company."*
>
> Psalm 55:14

Many people walked wherever they wanted to go. Walking was a handy way of traveling. A person could leave when he wanted. He could go just where he wanted. Can you think of any problems that a walking traveler might have?

Often a person wanted to take things with him when he traveled. Farmers wanted to take their crops to market. Fathers wanted to move their families to a new home. These people had to travel in the third way. They went by horse and wagon.

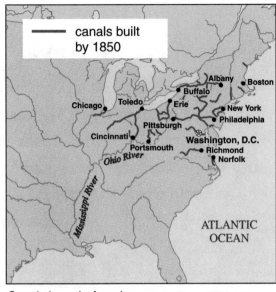

Canals in early America

People traveling by horse and wagon could not go as many places as people who walked. They followed roads and paths. The roads and paths in the early 1800s did not look like our paved roads. Most roads were dirt. What would happen to these dirt roads on a rainy day? People could not travel over the roads on days like that. They had to either find another way to travel or stay at home.

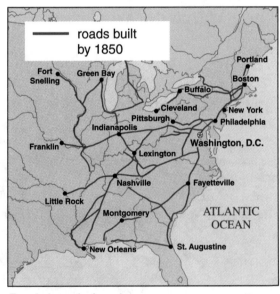

Roads in early America

The First Railroads

Do you think most people who lived in the early 1800s liked to travel? They did not. They wanted an easy *and* handy way to go from one place to another. What would you have done to make traveling better?

Some men thought of a plan. They would put wood or iron rails on the roads. The wagon wheels could roll along the rails. Then the wheels would not stick in the mud. It was a good plan. These rail roads made traveling handier and easier.

But the rail roads still were not perfect. The horses walked between the rails. Sometimes horses still got stuck in the mud. The travelers needed a better way to pull the wagons along the rail roads. Do you think they found a better way?

About the same time, men were making a new kind of boat. These boats had an engine that let them travel faster than other boats. This new engine even helped a boat travel up a river against the current. People called the boats *steamboats* because steam made the engine run. Could the same kind of engine pull a wagon?

Most people did not believe that steam-powered engines could pull wagons along the railroads. But some did. And one man built a small steam engine on wheels, a *locomotive*. Peter Cooper wanted to prove that a steam engine could pull wagons faster than horses could.

Cooper called his locomotive Tom Thumb. Why do you think he gave it that name? The men at the Baltimore and Ohio Railroad let Cooper test his little locomotive on their railroads. Tom Thumb raced a horse. Both Tom Thumb and the horse pulled wagons. Do you think Cooper's locomotive won the race?

Peter Cooper's locomotive, Tom Thumb

Building Model Railroads

Tiny *replicas,* or copies, of trains have been around almost as long as the full-sized ones. In the 1830s Mathias Baldwin made a model of a train. He wanted to show people his new locomotive design. Later, he built a full-sized train just like the model. He called the big locomotive Old Ironsides.

Big trains like Old Ironsides thrilled people of all ages. Soon companies began making little pull toy trains for children. Some toy trains came with track to pull or push the train around on.

Toy shops sold the first *working* toy trains about sixty years ago. The trains ran on tiny tracks carefully laid out on the floor. These working trains were popular toys. Soon older boys and girls, and even some adults, began working with the tiny trains. But they did not think of the trains as toys. They called them "model trains" instead.

Today there are many different sizes and kinds of model trains. You can buy a whole train set complete with train and tracks. Or you can buy one piece at a time. You can even buy a kit and build the locomotive and cars yourself. Some people still lay the track out on the floor and put it away each day. Others build elaborate railroads with mountains, rivers, bridges, and towns. Models like this can fill a whole room. Have you ever seen a model railroad that big?

How Railroads Worked

Steam made locomotives like Tom Thumb and Old Ironsides work. Do you know what happens when water turns to steam? It takes up more room. The steam presses on pipes inside the locomotive. It moves a special part that turns the wheels. Then the steam escapes through the smokestack. How do you think that part got its name?

Look at the diagram below. Can you find the water in this locomotive? We call that part the boiler because the water there is boiling hot.

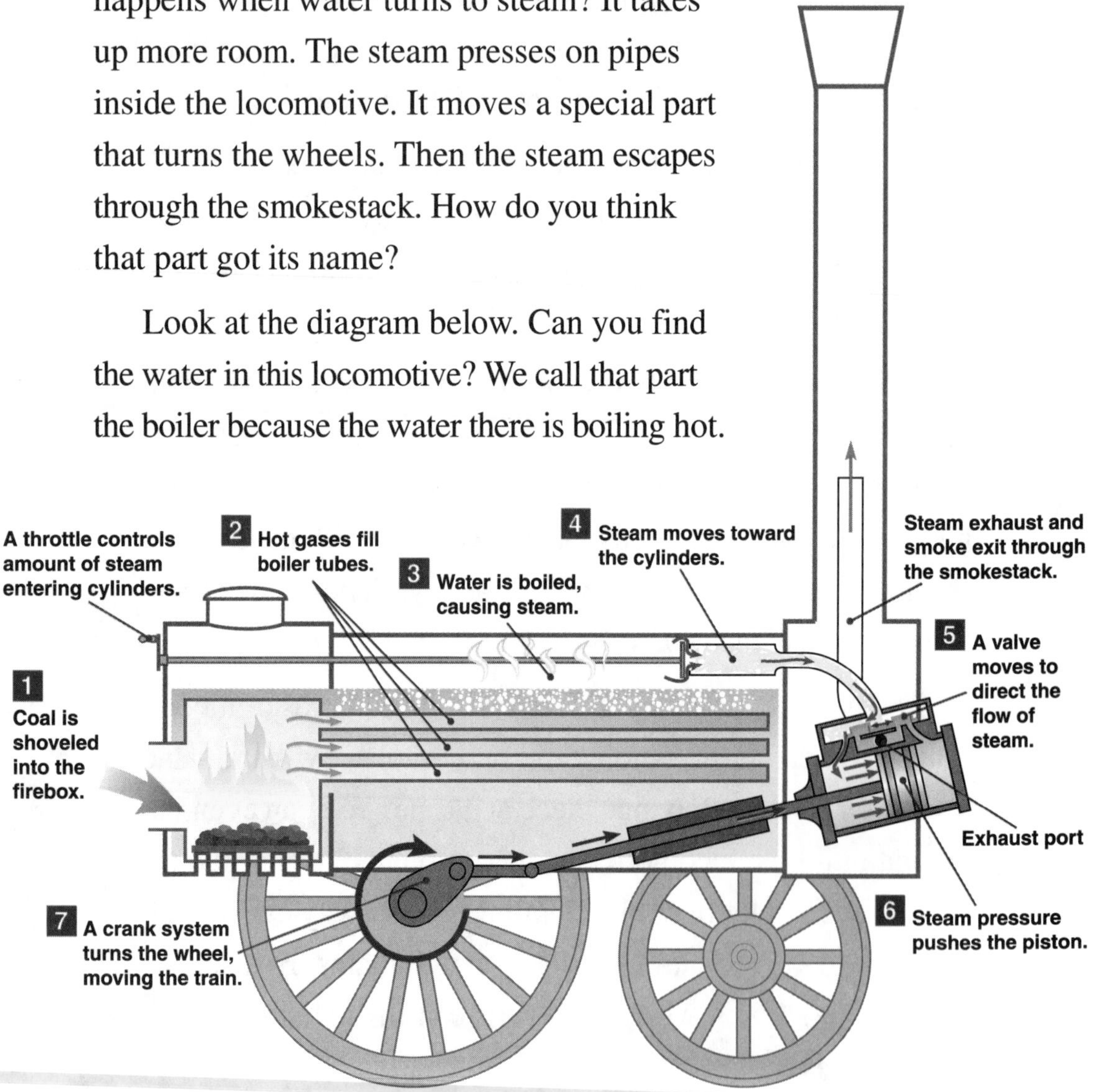

A throttle controls amount of steam entering cylinders.

2 Hot gases fill boiler tubes.

4 Steam moves toward the cylinders.

Steam exhaust and smoke exit through the smokestack.

3 Water is boiled, causing steam.

1 Coal is shoveled into the firebox.

5 A valve moves to direct the flow of steam.

Exhaust port

7 A crank system turns the wheel, moving the train.

6 Steam pressure pushes the piston.

How did the men running the locomotive make the water hot? What do you think they called the man who kept the fire burning?

The fireman had an important job. If he let the fire die down, the water would not be hot enough to keep the heavy train moving. If he shoveled too much coal into the firebox, the steam would build up too much. The train might travel too fast then. Or something even worse could happen. The boiler might blow up.

The fireman was not the only man who worked on the locomotive. The *engineer* was the boss on the train. He had to keep the train moving at a good speed. He had to watch the rails, or track, ahead. It was the engineer's job to bring the people and things on his train safely to the next town.

To Use a Map Scale

1. Get a large map of your state, a ruler, and Notebook page 79.

2. Look at the map on your Notebook page. It shows the area around Center Station. Find the scale on the map. According to the scale, how many miles does one inch equal?

3. Use your ruler to measure the distance from Center Station to End-of-Track. How far apart are the two places on the map? How many miles apart are they? Measure the distance to other points on the map. How far are they from Center Station in real distance?

4. Look at the map of your state. Can you find the scale on it? How many miles are equal to one inch on this map? Find your town on the map. Then use the scale to find the distance to the near-est large town. How far is it to the border of your state?

From Coast to Coast

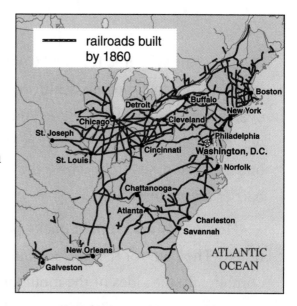

railroads built by 1860

Boston
Buffalo
Detroit
New York
Chicago
Cleveland
Philadelphia
St. Joseph
Cincinnati
Washington, D.C.
St. Louis
Norfolk
Chattanooga
Atlanta
Charleston
Savannah
New Orleans
ATLANTIC
Galveston
OCEAN

Railroads soon were a popular way to travel. Men laid out tracks to connect cities and towns from state to state. In 1830, when the first steam locomotives began running, there were only seventy-three miles of iron railroads. Just thirty years later, more than thirty thousand miles of track were ready to use. Most of the railroads were built in one part of the country. Can you tell which part by looking at the map?

President Lincoln knew that railroads would help the United States grow. Trains made travel easier. Trains carried *goods,* or things people needed and wanted, all over the eastern part of the country. When people decided to build a railroad in the West, President Lincoln wanted to help. How could a president help to build a railroad?

President Lincoln signed the Railroad Act of 1862. This act gave two companies the right to build the first *transcontinental* railroad. *Trans-* means "across." What other word do you see? What do you think *transcontinental* means? The Railroad Act promised the companies money and free land to put the track on.

The Central Pacific Railroad Company laid out tracks toward the east from Sacramento, California. These men began work even before the president signed the Railroad Act. Their work was slow and hard. A huge barrier stood in their path, less than one hundred miles from where they began. Can you find that barrier on the map?

How could the railroad tracks pass through a big mountain range? The path for the tracks wound back and forth, slowly climbing up the sides of the mountains. But in some places the sides were too steep. The men used dynamite and shovels to dig tunnels to the other side.

The Union Pacific Railroad Company's tracks began in Omaha, Nebraska. Can you find Omaha on the map? Their tracks headed west across the prairie. Do you think their work was as difficult as the work of the Central Pacific men? Because the land in Nebraska was flat, the Union Pacific men could work faster. They built more than one thousand miles of the railroad.

Promontory Point, Utah
May 10, 1869

The two railroad companies worked for almost eight years to build a railroad that crossed the country. They had laid 1,776 miles of track. Now just one set of thirty-foot rails was left.

Trains carried people all the way from Omaha and Sacramento. The companies planned a big celebration.

The companies made a special spike for the ceremony. It was not iron like all the other spikes. This spike was gold. The gold spike was the last one pounded into the rails. Men from each company took turns hitting the spike into place.

The two locomotives inched forward until their cowcatchers—metal grills— touched. The engineers shook hands. The transcontinental railroad was done!

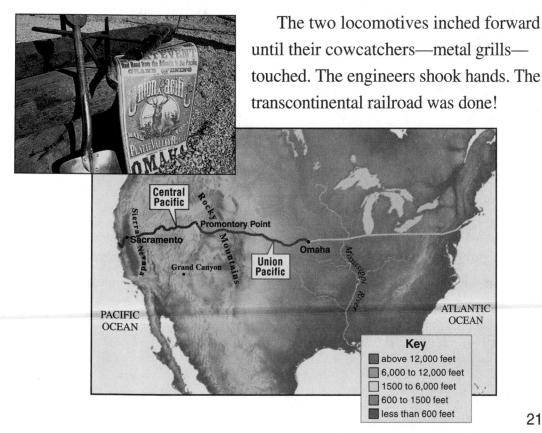

219

George Westinghouse
1846-1914

One man solved some of the railroad's worst problems. When he was a little boy, George Westinghouse worked in his father's machine shop. Before long he was trying to make new and different kinds of machines. He tested and rebuilt each new machine until it worked just the way he wanted it to. George Westinghouse made almost four hundred new machines, or *inventions.*

We remember George Westinghouse most for his invention called the *air brake.* Do you know what a brake is? A brake is a way to stop something. For many years, trains did not have good brakes. When an engineer saw that he must stop the train, he gave three toots on his whistle. When the brakeman heard the signal, he ran up and across the moving cars. He had to turn a wheel that set the brake on each car. The train would not stop until the brakeman turned every brake wheel. Sometimes the brakeman did not turn the brake wheels fast enough. What do you think happened then?

Westinghouse's air brake worked much faster. The engineer knew best when he needed to stop the train. He was the man who worked this new brake. The engineer turned one switch to set all the brakes. The train stopped!

Changes, for Better and Worse

Do you think travel by railroad was always safe? It was not. Sometimes the locomotives ran off the track. Sometimes the sparks from the smokestack set the wooden coaches on fire. Sometimes trains ran into animals, wagons, or even other trains stopped on the track. But it was still faster and more exciting than any other way of getting around.

As more and more trains used the new tracks, the railroads faced another problem. How could two trains travel in different directions on the same track? Unless someone thought of an answer, trains would always be in danger of running into each other.

Someone did find an answer. The railroads hired men to build *sidetracks* next to the main tracks. An engineer could pull his train onto the sidetrack to get out of the way of another train. The companies put a signal at each sidetrack. They put signals at other places too. The signals told the engineers when to stop on the sidetracks and when to keep going. Have you ever seen signals like these? What do they mean?

sidetrack

signal

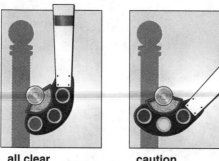
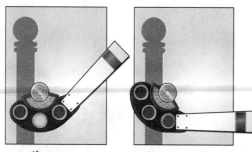

all clear   caution   stop

221

This signal system worked well when trains ran on time. But no one could agree on what the right time was. Each town set its clocks by the sun. One town's clock showed a little earlier time than the clock in the next town to the east. Sometimes an engineer left the station too soon, and people missed the train. Sometimes a train stayed in the station too long, and another train ran into it from behind.

Important men from each railroad company met in one place. They wanted to find a way to solve the time problem. The men decided to divide the U.S. map into four parts, or zones. Each part would have its own time. The time zones helped keep trains running on schedule. Soon people everywhere, not just on the railroad, set their clocks by the time zones.

Time Zones Work

1. Gather a flashlight, a globe, some Plasti-Tak, six clocks, and Notebook page 84.

2. Place the globe on a table. Put a bit of Plasti-Tak on the globe to show where you live. Darken the room. Pretend the flashlight is the sun and shine it on the globe right above the Plasti-Tak. What time is it at that spot on the globe? Slowly turn the globe to the east. Is the Plasti-Tak always right under the flashlight? In what part of the world is it noon now?

3. Set one of the clocks for the correct time where you are now. Then set the other clocks as your teacher tells you. Each clock represents the time it is now in a different part of the country, or time zone. Look at the map on your Notebook page. Can you find your state? Which time zone is it in?

Little by little, people found ways to solve the railroad's problems. Men found safe ways to stop fast-moving trains. Others thought of a safe way to *couple,* or join, the cars and locomotives. Companies built comfortable, pretty cars for people to ride in. New and bigger locomotives pulled long trains faster.

Today the railroads have a new problem. Few passenger trains travel across the United States. Faster, easier types of travel have taken their place. Do you know some of these new ways to travel?

Freight trains, or those that carry goods, still criss-cross the country. You might see an old steam locomotive in a museum or at a railroad yard. Would you like to ride on one of these trains?

You could probably ride a train similar to this one at your local zoo or amusement park.

12

The Wild West

What was so wild about the West anyway? Was it really a place of gunfighters and Indian raids and outlaws? Well, yes and no.

At the chuck wagon

The West did have some cattle thieves and a few shootouts and people who took the law into their own hands. But also in the West were honest ranchers and missionaries and Indians who wanted to live peaceably with the settlers.

There were good lawmen and a few bad lawmen. There were many farmers who plowed and reaped their fields year by year. There were soldiers and train robbers. There were schoolteachers and preachers, miners and mountain men. And there were lots of children.

A settler's daughter feeding the family's chickens

A roundup on a ranch in Kansas in 1902

A family in front of their sod house in Nebraska in 1886

This Nebraska homesteader also lived in a sod house.

Everyday Life

"Sod Busters" and Homesteaders

Tom woke up to a steady dripping on his face. He rolled over, and the water dropped on the floor beside his head. It had rained two days before. But the ceiling of the sod house was still "raining" inside. Another drop hit his ear. Tom got up.

His mother stood beside the low fire. She held an umbrella over the cooking. "Awake?" she said. "Papa wants you in the barn." A beetle ran out from the sod wall. Tom's mother smacked it with her hand.

In the barn, Tom's father was sharpening his scythe. "Morning," he said. "Soon as the sun dries things off, we'll get started." Tom nodded.

Tom drew water from the well for his mother. He glanced at the trees his father had planted three years before. Everyone had said that apple trees could not grow in the plains. But the thick leaves and the small round apples proved that they could.

If Tom's family could live here just two more years, the land would be theirs. Sometimes he thought that his mother would not make it. She cried when the cloth fell off the ceiling and dirt rolled all over. And she often was so tired that she would go to bed without even pulling back the covers.

Once he had seen his father cry. That was the day last summer when the locusts came. The huge insects had swarmed past. They made it dark in the middle of the day, there were so many. They made a roar, a horrible buzzing roar for hours. They ate every stalk and stem; they ruined everything that Tom's father had grown that whole summer.

But Tom's father had said, "If God wants us to have this land, He'll help us stay the five years." The *Homestead Act* promised settlers who lived on land five years that they could own that land. So Tom's parents did not give up. They were *homesteaders.*

But there was more trouble. Tom's father wanted to fence in some of the land. The ranchers to the south did not want the fence. They wanted to drive their cattle to market. They did not want to go around fences. They called his father a "sod buster." What do you think they meant?

Tom set the pail inside the door. "Here," said his mother. "Eat a biscuit before you go." Tom sat outside where it was dry and ate the biscuit. He prayed that there would be no locusts this year.

"The Lord redeemeth the soul of his servants: and none of them that trust in him shall be desolate."
Psalm 34:22

Ranchers

"Going up the Chisholm Trail?" The man threw a bedroll on the back of his saddle. "That's what I heard," said the other. He pulled the cinch on his saddle one more time. The two men got on their horses. They rode out to meet the *trail boss* and the other *cowboys*. They were setting out on a *cattle drive*.

The herd of cattle spread out before them like a sea. "Almost twenty-five hundred head," the trail boss told them. "We're heading up the old Chisholm Trail to Abilene. Head 'em up!" The cowboys swung out to the sides of the herd. The cattle drive was on.

Billy came behind with the extra horses. He was only four-teen, but he knew his job well. Horses liked him and he liked horses. Each of the nine cow-boys had eight or nine extra horses. About how many horses did Billy look after?

A modern cattle drive

Late at night, the cowboys on watch sometimes sang to the cattle to keep them quiet. One song was about the very trail they were on. What do you think the song is called? One night a thunderstorm came up. Lightning shot through the sky, and a crack of thunder shook the ground. Suddenly the cattle bolted into a run. "Ho!" yelled a cowboy. "Stampede!"

Everyone, even the cook, flew to the horses and took off after the cattle. They rode all night. In the morning, most of the cattle had stopped running. But many were scattered far and wide. The trail boss wiped his face on his sleeve. He shook his head. "It'll take a week to get them all back," he said.

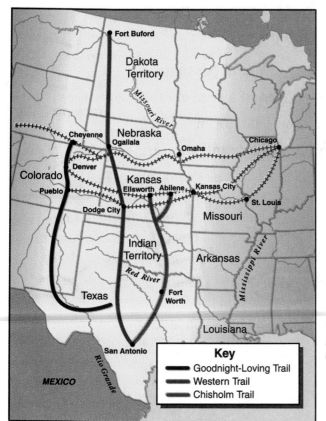

The cook made breakfast—beans and bacon and biscuits. He found some wild berries to throw in. But the food did not cheer the men up. The three-month trip had just gotten longer. Can you find the Chisholm Trail on the map?

This map shows the three major trails used when driving cattle to market.

How do you think the cowboys could tell their cattle from all the other herds in Abilene? Every ranch had its own *brand,* a mark the cowboys put on all the cattle. Ranchers branded their cattle so that thieves, called *rustlers,* could not take them and claim them. Look at the brands on this page. Can you tell how some of them got their names?

Walking 7

To brand the cattle, cowboys first had to catch them. Have you ever seen someone riding after a cow, swinging a loop of rope? That rope is the cowboy's *lariat.* The cowboy tried to get the loop around the cow's horns or neck. Once he got the cow stopped and down on the ground, he branded it.

Bar Y's

A *branding iron* was a piece of metal bent into a shape. The cowboys heated the iron in a fire and then pressed it onto the hip of the cow. The hot metal singed away the hair. The print of the brand was left on the hide.

Rocking chair

Lazy R

Bull head   Running W   Hat   Tumbling ladder

Sunrise

Holding Rodeos

When ranchers got together, they sometimes had contests. "I have a cowhand who can rope a calf quick as a wink," one might say. "I'd like to see that," another would say. The contests became yearly events. We call them *rodeos.*

Have you ever been to a rodeo? What did you like best—the calf roping, the bronco riding, or the bulldogging? The events at a rodeo are jobs that a cowboy had to do every day. Bronco riding came from breaking wild horses for riding. Bulldogging came from having to get a cow down to brand it.

Bulldogging, bringing down a steer by twisting its horns, was invented by Bill Pickett, the first black rodeo star. Bill was tall and strong. He could throw any steer. He became famous, traveling with rodeos all over the country. He even performed for Queen Victoria of England.

Calf roping

Bulldogging

Bronco riding

233

To Make Up a Brand

1. Get Notebook page 87 and a pencil.

2. Make up a name for your ranch. Mark the place on the map where your ranch is. Write the name beside the mark and in the key.

3. Draw the brand that your ranch will use. Keep it simple. Check with your "neighbors" to be sure your brand is not too much like theirs.

Ready for branding

Soldiers

Have you ever heard of the *cavalry?* The cavalry is the part of the United States Army that rode horses. The soldiers on this day had ridden fifteen miles. The dust rose from the dry ground. The saddles creaked, and horses snorted. Some men walked beside their horses to rest them.

The man with the bugle played a tune. Even the horses knew what the bugle tunes meant. This one told them that there was water to drink. The horses drank, and the men set up camp. After the horses were fed, supper was over, and the guns were cleaned, the bugle sang out "Taps." Have you ever heard that tune? It is played at funerals for soldiers. It signals that it is time to go to sleep.

Just as the sun came up the next morning, a band of Cheyenne rode down the ridge. They waved blankets and hollered at the horses. The horses started to jump and mill around. The soldier near the herd yelled, "They're after the horses!" The horses began to run. The bugler played "Stable Call" quickly. What do you think happened?

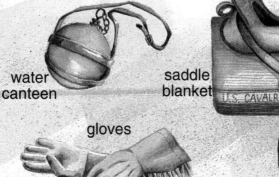

bridle

saddle

bugle

water
canteen

saddle
blanket

U.S. CAVALRY

gloves

The horses heard the tune and came back toward the camp. By now the soldiers had caught a few and were riding around the herd. The Cheyenne got away with only three. "Just three, sir," a soldier said. "Very well," said the sergeant. "Sound 'Mess Call.' " To the soldiers, *mess* meant a meal.

The soldiers would not go after three horses. They were on their way to defend a town. Soon they were riding, their saddles creaking. Sergeant Madsen waved his right hand back and forth over his head. The soldiers looked up. Then Madsen held up two fingers. The soldiers formed two lines. Why do you think the sergeant used hand signals?

To Follow Cavalry Signals

1. Get Notebook page 89.

2. Practice the hand signals on the page with your teacher.

3. As your teacher instructs, use the hand signals as though you were in the cavalry.

Lawmen

Another group of people who were trying to keep the peace in towns were the United States *marshals*. Marshals were like policemen of today. They tried to stop trouble. Sometimes they had to go after bank robbers and cattle thieves. Lawmen who took care of huge territories were called *sheriffs*. Most of the lawmen were good men.

Sergeant Madsen became a marshal after he left the cavalry. He was quiet, but he was a man to be respected. Once he trailed some bank robbers to a hideout. The robbers shot at him and ducked back into hiding. Madsen hollered for them to come out. They shot again. This time the marshal shot back. Madsen won. He was an expert with a rifle. He became famous for keeping the law in the West.

United States Marshal Chris Madsen

Frank and Jesse James
1843-1915 and 1847-82

Young Jesse James

There is more than one way to become famous. The James brothers chose the wrong way. The two had been Confederate soldiers in the Civil War. When they went home to Missouri, Frank and Jesse were rousted out at night by men with guns. The men wanted to arrest the brothers for what they had done during the war.

Soon after, the James brothers and some other men began robbing trains and banks. During the robberies, many people were shot and killed. Thousands and thousands of dollars were stolen. Always the gang of robbers got away—until three from the gang were killed and three more were captured in Minnesota.

Frank James when he was older

Frank and Jesse were never caught. Years later, Jesse was shot in the head by a man pretending to be his friend. Frank turned himself in to the law. He stood trial for robbery and murder. Surprisingly, there was universal sympathy for him because of the way Jesse was killed, and he was acquitted. He returned home and worked in a small Wild West show. He later died peaceably at home.

Native Americans

Spotted Tail, the great Sioux chief, sat in the circle, smoking a peace pipe. He nodded to the soldiers and glanced at the other chiefs with him. Then he signed the treaty. Now part of the lands of South Dakota belonged to the white men. The soldiers told him, "White men will stay out of your part of the land. It will always be yours." Spotted Tail nodded again, but he did not smile.

Chief Spotted Tail

When white men wanted land, they told the Sioux and others, "We'll make a deal with you." The signed papers said, "As long as the grass grows and the water flows, this part of the land will belong to the Sioux." For a few years the white men would keep their word. Then someone would discover gold or need more ranch land. What do you think happened to the treaties then?

A settler found gold in the hills of the Dakotas. Soon the white men forgot about the treaty with Spotted Tail. They ran the Native Americans off the land. "Find somewhere else to live," they said. "We need this land to hunt for gold." Some Sioux just left. Others said, "No more giving in. We will fight!"

Crazy Horse, Spotted Tail's nephew, wanted to fight. Sitting Bull, another Sioux chief, joined Crazy Horse. They gathered many warriors together. The United States government sent some cavalrymen to fight the Indians. The soldiers were led by Colonel George Armstrong Custer.

Custer was supposed to wait for more soldiers to join his men. "No," he said, "I need no help." He went into battle against hundreds of angry warriors at Little Bighorn. The soldiers were outnumbered and outfought. When the battle was over, not one of Custer's soldiers was standing.

The government sent more soldiers after Sitting Bull. They chased him into Canada. When he tried to come back to his people, he was caught. He went to live on a reservation. But still some Sioux did not give up hope.

Chief Sitting Bull

241

Wounded Knee Creek in the Dakota Badlands
December 29, 1890

A Paiute medicine man had said he had a vision. The vision told him that if his people would do the "ghost dance," they would get their lands back. If warriors wore "ghost shirts," no bullets could harm them.

The battleground at Wounded Knee

Many believed the medicine man. Why do you think they did? Sitting Bull said, "The ghost dance will bring back our hunting lands." The government feared what the Indians might do. The soldiers came to arrest Sitting Bull. They hurried him out, and he was shot.

The Indians fled the reservation. Cavalry soldiers chased them. Believing their ghost shirts would keep them safe, the Indians shot at the soldiers. The soldiers fired back. More than two hundred Indian men, women, and children were killed. The Sioux never fought back again.

The West Today

The fights over land, the gold rushes, and the Indian wars are over. Where many bison grazed are now farms. Fruit trees grow over the places that once held camps of cavalry soldiers. Factories and roads have been built where before were the fires of Sioux and Cheyenne tribes.

The prairie that once was so hard to get over in covered wagons is crossed with wide highways full of cars and tractor-trailers. The wind that once swept only grass now whips around houses and sky-scrapers and airports. What would the pioneers think if they saw their West today?

A family crossing the prairie in 1886

Cheyenne, Wyoming, in 1876

Modern San Antonio, Texas

But not all of the Old West is gone. The sense of freedom is there. And the spirit of independence is still strong. In the West even now, the grandchildren and the great-grandchildren of the pioneers are changing the West again, inventing and building and exploring different frontiers. Native Americans are regaining their long heritage. State parks are keeping some of the land the way it was in earlier days.

Monument Valley Tribal Park, Arizona

The United States has taken many ways of many peoples and made new ways from them. We call that way the *American way.* But America also allows people to keep their own culture. This freedom is also part of the American way. Since the days before Jamestown and Plymouth until today, the people in America have been thinkers and doers. All Americans would do well to learn from those earlier comers, to correct what is wrong and to keep what is right and good.

Merced River, Yosemite National Park

244

Resource
Treasury

Presidents

	President	Vice President	In Office	Political Party
1.	George Washington	John Adams	1789-97	None
2.	John Adams	Thomas Jefferson	1797-1801	Federalist
3.	Thomas Jefferson	Aaron Burr George Clinton	1801-9	Democratic-Republican
4.	James Madison	George Clinton Elbridge Gerry	1809-17	Democratic-Republican
5.	James Monroe	Daniel Tompkins	1817-25	Democratic-Republican
6.	John Q. Adams	John C. Calhoun	1825-29	Democratic-Republican
7.	Andrew Jackson	John C. Calhoun Martin Van Buren	1829-37	Democratic
8.	Martin Van Buren	Richard M. Johnson	1837-41	Democratic
9.	William H. Harrison	John Tyler	1841	Whig
10.	John Tyler		1841-45	Whig
11.	James K. Polk	George M. Dallas	1845-49	Democratic
12.	Zachary Taylor	Millard Fillmore	1849-50	Whig
13.	Millard Fillmore		1850-53	Whig
14.	Franklin Pierce	William R. King	1853-57	Democratic
15.	James Buchanan	John C. Breckinridge	1857-61	Democratic
16.	Abraham Lincoln	Hannibal Hamlin Andrew Johnson	1861-65	Republican, Union
17.	Andrew Johnson		1865-69	Union
18.	Ulysses S. Grant	Schuyler Colfax Henry Wilson	1869-77	Republican
19.	Rutherford B. Hayes	William A. Wheeler	1877-81	Republican
20.	James A. Garfield	Chester A. Arthur	1881	Republican
21.	Chester A. Arthur		1881-85	Republican
22.	Grover Cleveland	Thomas A. Hendricks	1885-89	Democratic
23.	Benjamin Harrison	Levi P. Morton	1889-93	Republican
24.	Grover Cleveland	Adlai E. Stevenson	1893-97	Democratic
25.	William McKinley	Garret A. Hobart Theodore Roosevelt	1897-1901	Republican
26.	Theodore Roosevelt	Charles W. Fairbanks	1901-9	Republican

President	Vice President	In Office	Political Party
27. William H. Taft	James S. Sherman	1909-13	Republican
28. Woodrow Wilson	Thomas R. Marshall	1913-21	Democratic
29. Warren G. Harding	Calvin Coolidge	1921-23	Republican
30. Calvin Coolidge	Charles G. Dawes	1923-29	Republican
31. Herbert Hoover	Charles Curtis	1929-33	Republican
32. Franklin D. Roosevelt	John N. Garner Henry A. Wallace Harry S Truman	1933-45	Democratic
33. Harry S Truman	Alben W. Barkley	1945-53	Democratic
34. Dwight D. Eisenhower	Richard M. Nixon	1953-61	Republican
35. John F. Kennedy	Lyndon B. Johnson	1961-63	Democratic
36. Lyndon B. Johnson	Hubert H. Humphrey	1963-69	Democratic
37. Richard M. Nixon	Spiro Agnew Gerald Ford	1969-74	Republican
38. Gerald Ford	Nelson Rockefeller	1974-77	Republican
39. Jimmy Carter	Walter Mondale	1977-81	Democratic
40. Ronald Reagan	George Bush	1981-89	Republican
41. George Bush	Dan Quayle	1989-93	Republican
42. Bill Clinton	Al Gore	1993-	Democratic

George Washington

1

1789-97

Born: February 22, 1732
Died: December 14, 1799

Place of birth: Westmoreland County, Virginia

Little-known fact: While president, he went to bed every night at nine o'clock.

John Adams

2

1797-1801

Born: October 30, 1735

Died: July 4, 1826

Place of birth: Braintree, Massachusetts

Little-known fact: He could read in seven languages.

Thomas Jefferson

3

1801-9

Born: April 13, 1743

Died: July 4, 1826

Place of birth: Shadwell, Virginia

Little-known fact: He had a pet mockingbird that ate crumbs from his lips.

James Madison

1809-17

Born: March 16, 1751
Died: June 28, 1836

Place of birth: Port Conway, Virginia
Little-known fact: He outlived all the other members of the Constitutional Convention.

James Monroe

1817-25

Born: April 28, 1758
Died: July 4, 1831

Place of birth: Westmoreland County, Virginia
Little-known fact: The capital of the country of Liberia is named for him—Monrovia.

John Quincy Adams

6

1825-29

Born: July 11, 1767

Died: February 23, 1848

Place of birth: Braintree, Massachusetts

Little-known fact: He was the first president to have his picture made with a camera.

Andrew Jackson

7

1829-37

Born: March 15, 1767

Died: June 8, 1845

Place of birth: Waxhaw, South Carolina

Little-known fact: He fought in the War for Independence at the age of thirteen.

Martin Van Buren

8

1837-41

Born: December 5, 1782
Died: July 24, 1862

Place of birth: Kinderhook, New York
Little-known fact: He was the first president to be born a
citizen of the United States rather than a British subject.

William Henry Harrison

9

**March 4, 1841–
April 4, 1841**

Born: February 9, 1773
Died: April 4, 1841

Place of birth: Berkeley, Virginia
Little-known fact: He had once studied medicine and
thought of becoming a doctor.

John Tyler

10

1841-45

Born: March 29, 1790
Died: January 18, 1862

Place of birth: Greenway, Virginia
Little-known fact: He was the first president to marry while in the White House.

James Knox Polk

11

1845-49

Born: November 2, 1795
Died: June 15, 1849

Place of birth: Mecklenburg County, North Carolina
Little-known fact: He signed a bill that created the Smithsonian Institution.

Zachary Taylor

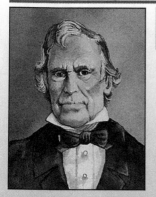

12

1849-50

Born: November 24, 1784

Died: July 9, 1850

Place of birth: Orange County, Virginia

Little-known fact: He was a cousin to James Madison.

Millard Fillmore

13

1850-53

Born: January 7, 1800

Died: March 8, 1874

Place of birth: Locke, New York

Little-known fact: He had the first bathtub put in the White House.

Franklin Pierce

14

1853-57

Born: November 23, 1804
Died: October 8, 1869

Place of birth: Hillsborough, New Hampshire
Little-known fact: He went to college with the famous
writers Nathaniel Hawthorne and Henry Wadsworth
Longfellow.

James Buchanan

15

1857-61

Born: April 23, 1791
Died: June 1, 1868

Place of birth: Cove Gap, Pennsylvania
Little-known fact: He was the only unmarried president.

Abraham Lincoln

16

1861-65

Born: February 12, 1809
Died: April 15, 1865

Place of birth: Hardin County, Kentucky
Little-known fact: He was the only president to hold a patent on an invention—a device to float ships over shoals.

Andrew Johnson

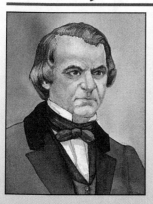

17

1865-69

Born: December 29, 1808
Died: July 31, 1875

Place of birth: Raleigh, North Carolina
Little-known fact: He was an expert tailor.

Ulysses Simpson Grant

18

1869-77

Born: April 27, 1822
Died: July 23, 1885

Place of birth: Point Pleasant, Ohio
Little-known fact: He set up the first national park—
Yellowstone.

Rutherford Birchard Hayes

19

1877-81

Born: October 4, 1822
Died: January 17, 1893

Place of birth: Delaware, Ohio
Little-known fact: He had the first telephone put in the
White House.

James Abram Garfield

20

**March 4, 1881–
September 19, 1881**

Born: November 19, 1831
Died: September 19, 1881

Place of birth: Orange, Ohio
Little-known fact: He could write with both hands at the same time—in different languages.

Chester Alan Arthur

21

1881-85

Born: October 5, 1829
Died: November 18, 1886

Place of birth: Fairfield, Vermont
Little-known fact: He was an excellent fisherman, once reeling in an eighty-pound bass.

Grover Cleveland

22

1885-89

Born: March 18, 1837
Died: June 24, 1908

Place of birth: Caldwell, New Jersey
Little-known fact: His daughter, Ruth, has a candy bar
  named after her—"Baby Ruth."

Benjamin Harrison

23

1889-93

Born: August 20, 1833
Died: March 13, 1901

Place of birth: North Bend, Ohio
Little-known fact: He was the last president to wear a beard.

Grover Cleveland

24

1893-97

Born: March 18, 1837
Died: June 24, 1908

Place of birth: Caldwell, New Jersey
Little-known fact: He was one of the hardest-working presidents, often staying up past 2 A.M. and sometimes even answering the White House phone himself.

William McKinley

25

1897-1901

Born: January 29, 1843
Died: September 14, 1901

Place of birth: Niles, Ohio
Little-known fact: He was the first president to use the telephone for campaign purposes.

Theodore Roosevelt

26

1901-9

Born: October 27, 1858

Died: January 6, 1919

Place of birth: New York, New York

Little-known fact: A metal eyeglass case prevented an assassin's bullet from entering his heart during a campaign speech for second term as president.

William Howard Taft

27

1909-13

Born: September 15, 1857

Died: March 8, 1930

Place of birth: Cincinnati, Ohio

Little-known fact: He was the last president to keep a cow on the White House lawn.

Woodrow Wilson

28

1913-21

Born: December 28, 1856
Died: February 3, 1924

Place of birth: Staunton, Virginia
Little-known fact: He loved golf so much that he would paint the balls black in order to play in the snow.

Warren Gamaliel Harding

29

1921-23

Born: November 2, 1865
Died: August 2, 1923

Place of birth: Corsica, Ohio
Little-known fact: Toothpicks were first introduced to the White House under his administration.

Calvin Coolidge

30

1923-29

Born: July 4, 1872
Died: January 5, 1933

Place of birth: Plymouth, Vermont

Little-known fact: Selective with both money and words, he was the most thrifty president—he even raised chickens on the White House yard.

Herbert Clark Hoover

31

1929-33

Born: August 10, 1874
Died: October 20, 1964

Place of birth: West Branch, Iowa

Little-known fact: His son, Allen, had two pet alligators that made themselves at home in the White House.

Franklin Delano Roosevelt

32

1933-45

Born: January 30, 1882
Died: April 12, 1945

Place of birth: Hyde Park, New York
Little-known fact: At age five, he met President Grover
Cleveland who stated, "I wish for you that you may never be
president."

Harry S Truman

33

1945-53

Born: May 8, 1884
Died: December 26, 1972

Place of birth: Lamar, Missouri
Little-known fact: In order to accommodate both
grandfathers, Solomon Young and Anderson Shippe Truman,
Harry Truman's full middle name is "S" without a period.

Dwight David Eisenhower

34

1953-61

Born: October 14, 1890

Died: March 28, 1969

Place of birth: Denison, Texas

Little-known fact: His nickname throughout life was "Ike." Even during his campaigns, crowds would shout, "We like Ike!"

John Fitzgerald Kennedy

35

1961-63

Born: May 29, 1917

Died: November 22, 1963

Place of birth: Brookline, Massachusetts

Little-known fact: At age forty-three, he was the youngest man ever elected president.

Lyndon Baines Johnson

36

1963-69

Born: August 27, 1908

Died: January 22, 1973

Place of birth: Stonewall, Texas

Little-known fact: In the first grade, he boasted that he would be president someday.

Richard Milhous Nixon

37

1969-74

Born: January 9, 1913

Died: April 22, 1994

Place of birth: Yorba Linda, California

Little-known fact: His beard grew so fast that he had to shave two to three times a day.

Gerald Rudolph Ford

38

1974-77

Born: July 14, 1913
Died: —

Place of birth: Omaha, Nebraska
Little-known fact: He needed only four hours of sleep each night.

James Earl Carter

39

1977-81

Born: October 1, 1924
Died: —

Place of birth: Plains, Georgia
Little-known fact: He was the first president to run a TV talk show. "Ask Mr. Carter" ran for two hours with forty-two out of nine million callers getting through for each show.

Ronald Wilson Reagan

40

1981-89

Born: February 6, 1911

Died: —

Place of birth: Tampico, Illinois

Little-known fact: At age sixty-nine, he was the oldest man ever elected president.

George Herbert Walker Bush

41

1989-93

Born: June 12, 1924

Died: —

Place of birth: Milton, Massachusetts

Little-known fact: He was named after his grandfather, "Pop"; therefore, his nickname was "Poppy" (little Pop).

William Jefferson Clinton

42

1993-

Born: August 19, 1946

Died: —

Place of birth: Hope, Arkansas

Little-known fact: He was born William Jefferson Blythe IV. At age fifteen, he had his name formally changed to William Jefferson Clinton, after his stepfather's last name.

Signs of Freedom

The Flags So Far

Many flags have flown over the United States. Here are the ones that flew before the American Civil War.

The Grand Union flag, or Cambridge flag

Two versions of the flag of 1777

The flag of 1795

Two versions of the flag of 1818

The flag of 1861

The Great Seal

This sign appears on all important papers of the United States government.

The eagle and the shield stand for independence.

These words mean "from many, one." How is that a good saying for the seal of the United States?

The olive branch stands for peace.

The arrows mean that the United States is not afraid to make war.

The National Bird

Benjamin Franklin wanted the turkey to be the bird of the United States. He said that it would "attack . . . the British Guards, who should invade his farmyard with a red coat on."

But other people thought the eagle was a better symbol for the United States. The eagle is mighty and beautiful.

In 1782, Congress voted for the eagle to be the national bird.

The Constitution of the United States
Preamble

We the people of the United States, in order to form a more perfect union, establish justice, insure domestic tranquility, provide for the common defense, promote the general welfare, and secure the blessings of liberty to ourselves and our posterity, do ordain and establish this Constitution for the United States of America.

Articles of the Constitution

Articles are the parts of the Constitution that describe the workings of the federal and state governments. The seven articles set forth a general plan that tells how the United States government should be organized.

Articles I through III discuss the three parts of the federal government: the legislative, the executive, and the judicial branches. Article IV outlines the relationships of the states with each other and with the federal government. Articles V and VII describe the processes of amending and ratifying the Constitution. Article VI discusses the handling of the national debt that existed prior to the writing of the Constitution. These seven articles precede the Bill of Rights.

Bill of Rights

1. Freedoms of religion, of speech, of the press, and of assembly and petition
2. Right to bear arms
3. Limits on the housing of soldiers
4. Limits on searches and seizures
5. Right to due process of law
6. Rights of a person accused of a crime
7. Right to a jury trial in civil cases
8. Forbidding of unfair bail, fines, and punishment
9. Rights not listed in the Constitution given to citizens
10. Powers reserved to the states or the people

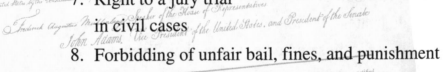

Lincoln immediately after he gave his speech at Gettysburg

The Gettysburg Address

President Lincoln spoke these words at the dedication of the Gettysburg cemetery. Many people thought his speech was too short. But it told how he felt about the brave soldiers in both armies.

Four score and seven years ago our fathers brought forth on this continent, a new nation, conceived in Liberty, and dedicated to the proposition that all men are created equal.

Now we are engaged in a great civil war, testing whether that nation, or any nation so conceived and so dedicated, can long endure. We are met on a great battlefield of that war. We have come to dedicate a portion of that field as a final resting place for those who here gave their lives that that nation might live. It is altogether fitting and proper that we should do this.

But in a larger sense we can not dedicate—we can not consecrate—we can not hallow—this ground. The brave men, living and dead, who struggled here, have consecrated it, far above our poor power to add or detract. The world will little note, nor long remember what we say here, but it can never forget what they did here. It is for us the living, rather to be dedicated here to the unfinished work which they who fought here have thus far so nobly advanced. It is rather for us to be here dedicated to the great task remaining before us—that from these honored dead we take increased devotion to that cause for which they gave the last full measure of devotion—that we here highly resolve that these dead shall not have died in vain—that this nation, under God, shall have a new birth of freedom—and that government of the people, by the people, for the people, shall not perish from the earth.

Lincoln's hand-written copy of the Gettysburg Address looked like this.

Special Days

Arbor Day

Every year, some states make one day a tree-planting day. The day is called *Arbor Day* because *arbor* means "tree."

The first Arbor Day was April 10, 1872, in Nebraska. Soon other states began to hold Arbor Days. Does your state?

Thanksgiving

The Pilgrims and Native Americans celebrated a thanksgiving day in 1621. But Thanksgiving was not always celebrated at harvest time. And it was not celebrated every year until 1863.

The Thanksgiving celebrations begun in 1863 by Abraham Lincoln gave Americans the tradition of eating turkey on the last Thursday of November.

Traditions

George Washington's Cherry Tree

One of the most famous stories about George Washington is just that—a story. There is no proof that George Washington chopped down his father's cherry tree and owned up to doing it. A man named Mason Weems made up that tale. But it has been told for so many years and it seems so much like what honest George would have done, that many people think the story is true.

Ancient Peoples

Many of the methods of modern people come from the ways of people who lived long before. The Pima and Papago peoples have irrigation systems like those of the Hohokam people, who lived in the southwestern United States before Christ was born. The Hopi and Zuni people living by the Rio Grande have houses very much like the Anasazi people who lived there hundreds of years ago.

Ruins of ancient Anasazi houses

Modern Hopi houses

Maps

World: Political

ARCTIC OCEAN

BEAUFORT SEA

Baffin Bay

GREENLAND

GREEN
SEA

ICELAND

BERING SEA

Gulf of Alaska

Hudson Bay

LABRADOR SEA

IRELA

CANADA

English Cha

NORTH ATLANTIC OCEAN

Bay of Bi

PORTUGAL

U. S. A.

NORTH PACIFIC OCEAN

CANARY ISLANDS

MOROC

MEXICO

Gulf of Mexico

THE BAHAMAS

WESTERN
SAHARA

CUBA

MAURITANIA

BELIZE

JAMAICA

HAITI

DOM. REP.

SENEGAL

GUATEMALA

HONDURAS

MAL

GAMBIA

EL SALVADOR

NICARAGUA

CARIBBEAN SEA

GUINEA BISSAU

GUINEA

COSTA RICA

SIERRA LEONE

PANAMA

VENEZUELA

LIBERIA

GUYANA

BUF
FA

SURINAME

COLOMBIA

FRENCH GUIANA

ECUADOR

PERU

BRAZIL

BOLIVIA

CHILE

PARAGUAY

SOUTH PACIFIC OCEAN

SOUTH ATLANTIC OCEAN

ARGENTINA

URUGUAY

FALKLAND ISLANDS

SOUTH GEORGIA ISLAND

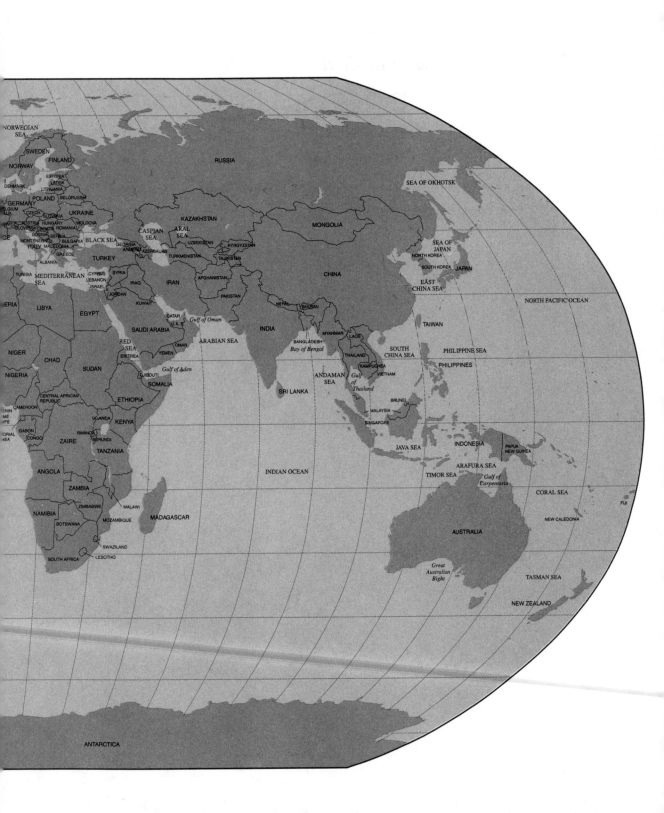

The United States: Political

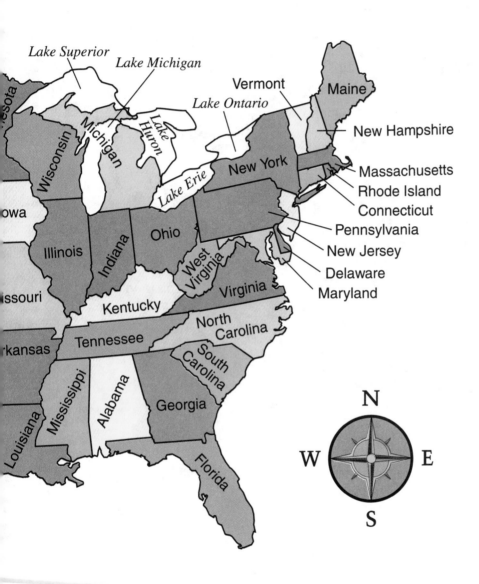

Lake Superior
Lake Michigan
Vermont
Maine
Lake Ontario
New Hampshire
Lake Huron
Michigan
Lake Erie
New York
Massachusetts
Rhode Island
Connecticut
Pennsylvania
New Jersey
Delaware
Maryland
Minnesota
Wisconsin
Iowa
Illinois
Indiana
Ohio
West Virginia
Virginia
Missouri
Kentucky
Arkansas
Tennessee
North Carolina
South Carolina
Mississippi
Alabama
Georgia
Louisiana
Florida

N
W   E
S

Hawaii

The United States: Physical

Washington
Olympia ● ▲ Mt. Rainier
▲ Mt. St. Helens
● Salem

North Dakota
● Bismarck

Oregon

Helena ●

Montana

South Dakota
Pierre ●

Boise ●

Idaho

Rocky Mountains

Wyoming

Black Hills

Nevada

Carson City ●

Salt Lake City ●

Cheyenne ●

Nebraska
Platte River

Sacramento ●

Sierra Nevada

Utah

Denver ●
▲ Pikes Peak

Linc

California

Grand Canyon

Colorado

Kansas
Arkansas River

Arizona

Santa Fe ●

Oklahoma

PACIFIC OCEAN

Phoenix ●

New Mexico

Oklahoma City ●

Red River

Texas

Austin ●

Rio Grande

Honolulu ●

Hawaii

same scale as large map

Yukon River

Alaska

Juneau ●

0 100 200 300 400 500
scale in miles

284

Indian Nations of Long Ago

The American Indians have truly earned the title Native Americans, for they have been in the Americas for thousands of years. As settlers from other places spread from coast to coast, Native American territory shrank, driving many groups onto reservations.

Key

#	Group	#	Group	#	Group
1.	Aleut	12.	Iroquois	23.	Yuma
2.	Eskimo	13.	Nez Perce	24.	Navajo
3.	Hare	14.	Sioux	25.	Hopi
4.	Dogrib	15.	Fox	26.	Comanche
5.	Tlingit	16.	Potawatomi	27.	Kiowa
6.	Nootka	17.	Tolowa	28.	Caddo
7.	Chippewyan	18.	Shoshone	29.	Natchez
8.	Cree	19.	Crow	30.	Choctaw
9.	Lillouet	20.	Pawnee	31.	Seminole
10.	Blackfoot	21.	Shawnee	32.	Carib
11.	Algonquin	22.	Pedee	33.	Arawak

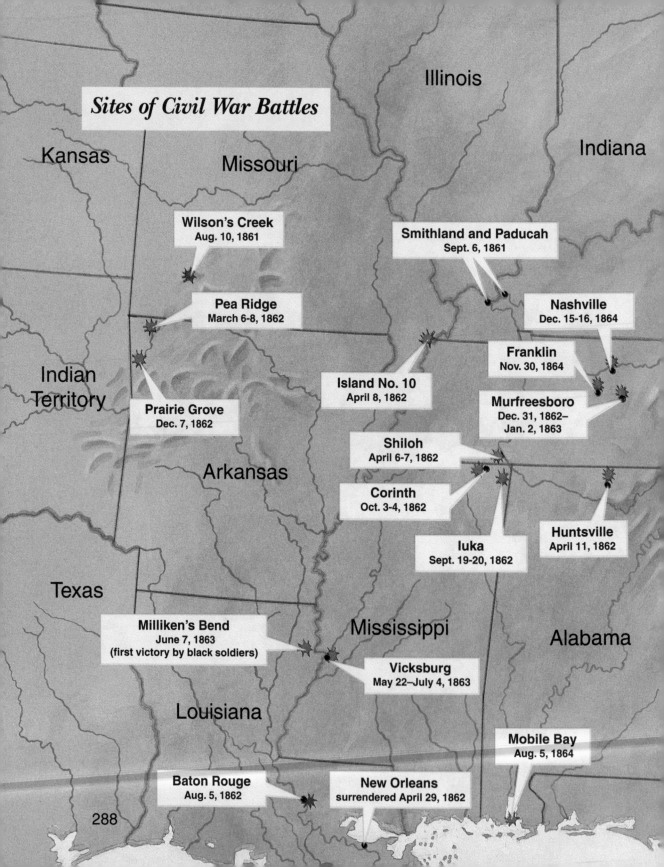

Sites of Civil War Battles

Kansas

Missouri

Illinois

Indiana

Wilson's Creek
Aug. 10, 1861

Smithland and Paducah
Sept. 6, 1861

Nashville
Dec. 15-16, 1864

Pea Ridge
March 6-8, 1862

Franklin
Nov. 30, 1864

Indian Territory

Island No. 10
April 8, 1862

Murfreesboro
Dec. 31, 1862–
Jan. 2, 1863

Prairie Grove
Dec. 7, 1862

Shiloh
April 6-7, 1862

Arkansas

Corinth
Oct. 3-4, 1862

Huntsville
April 11, 1862

Iuka
Sept. 19-20, 1862

Texas

Milliken's Bend
June 7, 1863
(first victory by black soldiers)

Mississippi

Alabama

Vicksburg
May 22–July 4, 1863

Louisiana

Mobile Bay
Aug. 5, 1864

288

Baton Rouge
Aug. 5, 1862

New Orleans
surrendered April 29, 1862

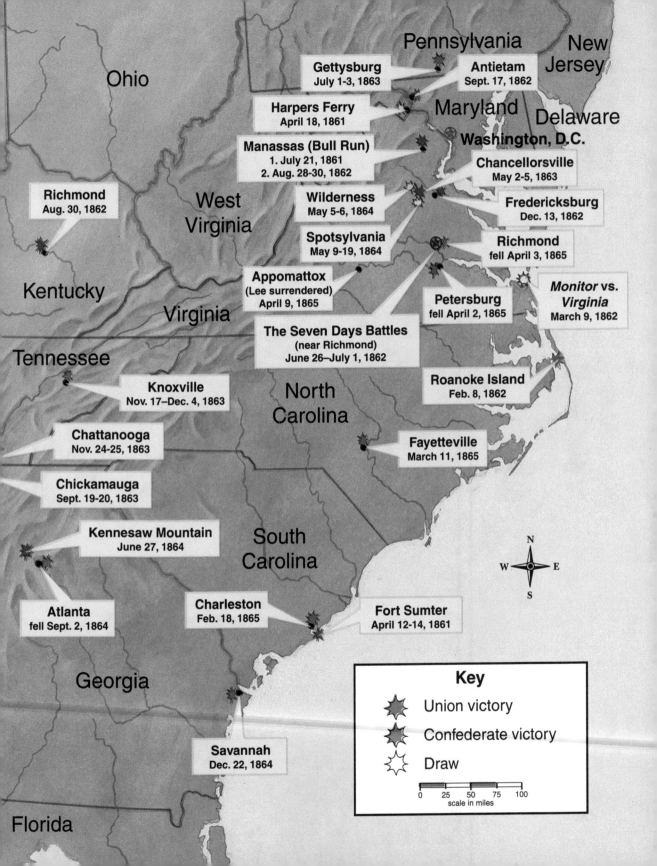

Geogloss

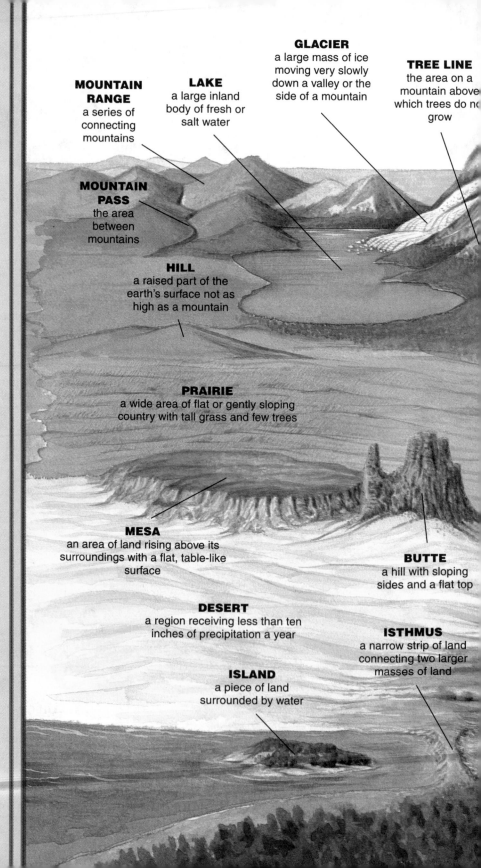

MOUNTAIN RANGE
a series of connecting mountains

LAKE
a large inland body of fresh or salt water

GLACIER
a large mass of ice moving very slowly down a valley or the side of a mountain

TREE LINE
the area on a mountain above which trees do no grow

MOUNTAIN PASS
the area between mountains

HILL
a raised part of the earth's surface not as high as a mountain

PRAIRIE
a wide area of flat or gently sloping country with tall grass and few trees

MESA
an area of land rising above its surroundings with a flat, table-like surface

BUTTE
a hill with sloping sides and a flat top

DESERT
a region receiving less than ten inches of precipitation a year

ISTHMUS
a narrow strip of land connecting two larger masses of land

ISLAND
a piece of land surrounded by water

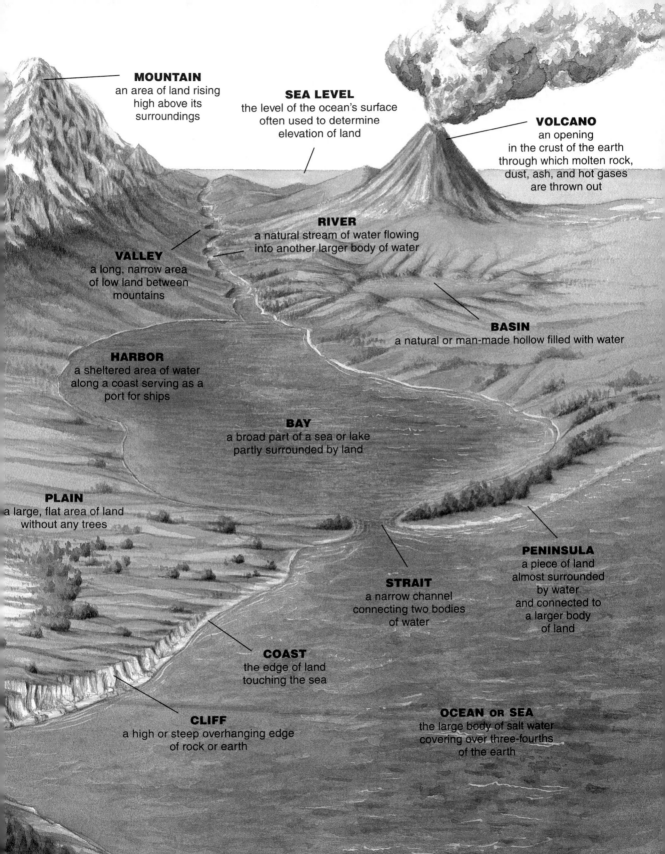

MOUNTAIN
an area of land rising
high above its
surroundings

SEA LEVEL
the level of the ocean's surface
often used to determine
elevation of land

VOLCANO
an opening
in the crust of the earth
through which molten rock,
dust, ash, and hot gases
are thrown out

RIVER
a natural stream of water flowing
into another larger body of water

VALLEY
a long, narrow area
of low land between
mountains

BASIN
a natural or man-made hollow filled with water

HARBOR
a sheltered area of water
along a coast serving as a
port for ships

BAY
a broad part of a sea or lake
partly surrounded by land

PLAIN
a large, flat area of land
without any trees

PENINSULA
a piece of land
almost surrounded
by water
and connected to
a larger body
of land

STRAIT
a narrow channel
connecting two bodies
of water

COAST
the edge of land
touching the sea

CLIFF
a high or steep overhanging edge
of rock or earth

OCEAN OR SEA
the large body of salt water
covering over three-fourths
of the earth

Glossary

ambassador one chosen to represent his government to another government

amendment a change, addition, or improvement

Articles of Confederation the first constitution of the American colonies; replaced by the present Constitution

Bill of Rights a list of freedoms added to the Constitution; the first ten amendments

capital the main city of a country or state

compromise *(kom'prə·mīz')* an idea that is not exactly what either side wants but is good enough for both sides to like

Confederate States of America a group of eleven states that tried to make themselves a separate country

Constitution the main laws of the United States

Constitutional Convention a meeting called to write the laws for the United States

continent one of the seven largest pieces of land on the earth

Easter the day Christians celebrate Christ's resurrection

Emancipation Proclamation a paper signed by Abraham Lincoln, freeing the slaves in the Confederate states

folk song a tune with words sung by people from generation to generation and having no known author

folktale a story told by common people for generations

gold rush the sudden and large migration to California where gold had been found

goods items that people need or want

homesteader one who claims land and builds on it

House of Burgesses a lawmaking body of colonial Virginia

Independence Hall a building in Philadelphia in which the Declaration of Independence and the Constitution were written

invention a new device or way of doing something

liberty the freedom to do and say what one thinks is right

Mayflower the ship that brought Separatists and others to the New World

Mayflower Compact an agreement signed by some men on the *Mayflower* to help set up a government in Plymouth Plantation

national anthem the official song of a country

Oregon Trail a major route to the West in the 1840s

physical map a map showing parts of the earth's surface, such as rivers, mountains, and so on

Preamble the opening part of the Constitution

Presidents' Day a day in February for honoring Presidents Washington and Lincoln

ratify to agree to or approve

right something that is due to a person by law or nature

Sacajawea the Shoshone woman who was a guide for Lewis and Clark

Senate one of the two houses of Congress

slave a person bought by others and made to work for no money when he does not want to

surveyor one who measures land

territory land that the United States owns but has not made a state

"The Star-Spangled Banner" the national anthem of the United States

time zone an area in which all clocks are set to the same time

Trail of Tears the hard journey of a Cherokee tribe from Georgia to Oklahoma

transcontinental crossing a continent

Underground Railroad the secret route from the slave states to Canada by which slaves escaped

Union the United States

War of 1812 fight between England and the United States; begun when American sailors were kidnapped by England

Wilderness Road one of the important roads from east to west in pioneer times

INDEX

A

abolitionists, 139, 141, 145, 177
Adams, John Quincy, 126, 246, 250
Alamo, 135-36
amendment, 189
Appleseed, Johnny, 96-99
Arawaks. *See* Native Americans
Articles of Confederation, 6, 9, 15

B

Beckwourth, James, 66
Bleeding Kansas, 142, 145
Bonaparte, Napoleon, 42, 71
Boone, Daniel, 64
Booth, John Wilkes, 190
Brady, Mathew, 178

C

camp meetings, 84-85
cavalry, 235, 237-38, 241-43
Central Pacific Railroad Company, 218-19
Cherokee. *See* Native Americans
Cheyenne. *See* Native Americans
Christmas, 205
circuit-riding preacher, 84
Civil War (American), 163, 166, 169, 180, 185-86, 190, 194, 197, 239
Clark, William, 57-59, 61-62, 116
Clay, Henry, 72, 133, 138, 142

Columbus, Christopher, 119, 202-3
Columbus Day, 202
Confederacy. *See* Confederate States of America
Confederate States of America, 147-48, 160, 162, 166-68, 170-73, 176, 179, 182, 187, 189
Constitution, 9, 14-18, 20-22, 24, 34, 129-30, 189
Constitutional Convention, 6, 14, 115
Coolidge, Calvin, 247, 262
Coronado, 119
cotton gin, 130-31
cowboys, 154, 230-33

D

Declaration of Independence, 34, 126

E

Easter, 196
Emancipation Proclamation, 179, 181, 189

F

fable, 91, 100, 104
folk songs, 154
folktale, 101, 104
Fort Sumter, 148, 166
Foster, Stephen, 151
Fourth of July, 200
Franklin, Benjamin, 7, 17, 34
French Revolution, 34, 37, 41

Photograph Credits

The following agencies and individuals have furnished materials to meet the photographic needs of this textbook. We wish to express our gratitude to them for their important contribution.

Suzanne R. Altizer
George R. Buckley
Capitol Preservation Committee
Chessie System Railroads
George R. Collins
Corel Corporation
Terry M. Davenport
Dave Fisher
Illinois State Historical Library
Brian D. Johnson
Library of Congress
Ray Manley
R. J. McDaniel
Mt. Vernon Ladies Association
National Archives
National Gallery of Art

National Park Service
Nebraska Department of
    Economic Development
Nebraska State Historical Society
J. Norman Powell
Wade K. Ramsey
Reunion des Musees Nationaux
Karen Rowe
Salt Lake Convention and
    Visitors Bureau
South Dakota State Historical
    Society
Stock Montage, Inc.
Texas Tourist Development
    Agency
United States Air Force

United States Department of
    Agriculture (USDA)
United States Department of
    Transportation
United States Fish and Wildlife
    Service
Unusual Films
Brian Vogt
Ward's Natural Science
    Establishment
Dawn L. Watkins
The White House
Woolaroc Museum
Worldwide Slides
Yellowstone National Park
Zion National Park

Cover
Dawn L. Watkins (top, left); Texas Tourist Development Agency (bottom)

Title Page
Brian D. Johnson

Chapter 1
National Park Service 1; George R. Collins 2, 6, 12; National Archives 5; Capitol Preservation Committee and Brian Hunt of Hunt Commercial Photography 7, 17; Library of Congress 9; Unusual Films 13, 14, 18 (bottom), 19, 22; Official White House Photo 18 (top)

Chapter 2
Unusual Films 23, 40; Library of Congress 25, 42 (top); National Archives 26; Reunion des Musees Nationaux 32; Worldwide Slides 35; National Gallery of Art 42 (bottom)

Chapter 3
George R. Collins 43, 44 (center, right), 48-49, 54 (background), 62; U.S. Department of Transportation 44 (left); Unusual Films 47; National Park Service 48 (right), 50 (top), 53 (all); U.S. Fish and Wildlife Service 48 (center); Brian

Vogt 48 (left); Brian D. Johnson 50-51, 51; George R. Buckley 50 (center top, center bottom); Nebraska Department of Economic Development 50 (bottom); J. Norman Powell 52 (background); Zion National Park 52 (top); Corel Corporation 52 (bottom); Ward's Natural Science Establishment 53 (background)

Chapter 4
George R. Collins 63, 64 (top); Yellowstone National Park 64 (bottom); Unusual Films 69, 76, 84, 85; Library of Congress 80; Salt Lake Convention and Visitors Bureau 81; Woolaroc Museum, Bartlesville, OK 82; George R. Buckley 88 (bottom); South Dakota State Historical Society 88 (top)

Chapter 5
Unusual Films 89, 100, 108

Chapter 6
Brian D. Johnson 109; George R. Collins 111; National Park Service 113, 119; Wade K. Ramsey 114; Library of Congress 115; Unusual Films 118, 121, 123; Karen Rowe 124 (both); Terry M. Davenport 126

Chapter 7
Library of Congress 127, 129, 139, 140, 144 (both), 145 (right), 148 (center, bottom); R. J. McDaniel 137; Illinois State Historical Library 145 (left); Unusual Films 146; National Park Service 148 (top)

Chapter 8
Library of Congress 151 (both); Unusual Films 153, 156 (both), 162

Chapter 9
Unusual Films 165; Corel Corporation 170; National Archives 172, 178 (bottom left); Library of Congress 174 (both), 176, 178 (top, bottom right), 179, 186, 187, 188, 190 (both); National Park Service 177, 185; Stock Montage, Inc. 181

Chapter 10
Unusual Films 191, 192, 199 (both), 201, 205 (left, right); Mt. Vernon Ladies Association 193; Library of Congress 194; Wade K. Ramsey 195 (right); Dave Fisher 195 (left); Suzanne R. Altizer 197; United States Air Force 200; George R. Collins 205 (center)

Chapter 11
National Park Service 207, 219; Chessie System Railroads 212; Unusual Films 213, 216, 223, 224; Library of Congress 220

Chapter 12
George R. Collins 225; Nebraska State Historical Society 226 (bottom right); National Archives 226 (center, bottom left), 243 (top, center); Solomon D. Butcher Collection, Nebraska State Historical Society 227; Texas Tourist Development Agency 230 (both); Corel Corporation 233 (all); USDA 234; Unusual Films 237; Library of Congress 239 (both), 240, 241; South Dakota State Historical Society 242; Ray Manley 244 (top); National Park Service 244 (bottom)

Resource Treasury
Dawn L. Watkins 245; The White House 268; National Park Service 271; Unusual Films 272-73, 276; Library of Congress 274; Corel Corporation 279 (bottom); Terry M. Davenport 279 (top)